Greek Mythology

A Stunning Journey Through Ages and Timeless
Stories. Discover the Mystery, the Charm of Gods,
Heroes, and Ancient Legends that Shaped Civilization

Xander Liosis

INKWELL
HOUSE PRESS

Summary

INTRODUCTION

Welcome! As you embark on this awe-inspiring journey into the realms of Greek mythology, prepare to be enthralled by tales of mighty heroes, capricious gods, and fantastical creatures that have inspired generations of storytellers, artists, and philosophers. This book is a ticket to an enchanting world filled with adventure, love, tragedy, and magic—a world that has shaped the very foundations of human culture and continues to enthrall us today.

In addition to the captivating myths themselves, we will delve into the historical background of ancient Greece, shedding light on the fascinating culture that birthed these enduring stories. You'll gain a deeper understanding of the Greek way of thinking and the societal norms that shaped their world, allowing you to fully appreciate the complexities and nuances of these timeless tales.

As we explore the impact of Greek mythology on modern society, you'll come to see how its themes and motifs continue to resonate in contemporary art, literature, and philosophy. The ancient Greeks' insights into human nature, love, power, and the cosmic order still hold relevance today, providing valuable lessons that can guide us on our own journeys through life.

As you delve into these pages, you'll come face to face with Zeus, the almighty god of the sky and thunder, whose powerful presence has echoed through the ages. You'll meet Athena, the goddess of wisdom, whose unyielding pursuit of knowledge and justice has inspired countless mortals to strive for greatness. And you'll witness the passion and fury of Poseidon, god of the sea, whose mighty trident can conjure storms and send tremors rippling across the earth.

But Greek mythology isn't just about the gods. It's also about the intrepid heroes who dared to challenge fate and embark on harrowing journeys to prove their valor. You'll cheer on Hercules as he faces twelve seemingly impossible labors, and follow Theseus into the heart of the Labyrinth as he confronts the fearsome Minotaur. Along the way, you'll meet other legendary figures like Ulysses, Achilles, and Jason, whose stories have been retold countless times and have become synonymous with courage, ingenuity, and triumph.

Greek mythology is not just a collection of stories—it's a living, breathing tapestry of human experience. Each myth is a testament to the boundless creativity and insight of the ancient Greeks, who used these tales to explore the nature of the human condition, the complexities of love and power, and the eternal struggle between order and chaos. As you immerse yourself in this mesmerizing world, you'll come to appreciate how these myths have served as a wellspring of inspiration for artists, poets, and thinkers throughout history, and how they can enrich our lives even today.

As you turn these pages, we invite you to let your imagination soar, as you uncover the hidden meanings and universal truths that lie beneath the surface of these ancient tales. You're about to embark on an unforgettable odyssey into the heart of Greek mythology—a realm where gods walk among mortals, where heroes defy the impossible, and where epic battles decide the fate of the cosmos.

Welcome, dear reader, to the world of Greek mythology. May your journey be filled with wonder, wisdom, and above all, good reading!

CHAPTER 1
The Greeks - Where Did They Come From?

Ah, the ancient Greeks, an extraordinary civilization that has left us with tales of derring-do, love, and divine mischief. But where did these enigmatic people come from, and how did their mythologies come to be? It's a tale as intriguing as the myths themselves.

You see, the Greeks had quite a colorful history, and their vibrant myths were shaped by numerous influences from far and wide. Invaders from distant lands, such as Asia Minor, swooped in like Hermes on a particularly zippy day and left their mark on Greek culture. Moreover, the Greeks' interactions with other ancient civilizations—like the Babylonians and the Sumerians—spiced up their stories like a pinch of Mediterranean oregano.

Enter Homer, the legendary bard who was part philosopher, part wordsmith, and (let's be honest) part rock star of his time. Most of his epic works, which have stood the test of time, were crafted between 750 and 700 BC. It's thanks to his prolific quill that we have a treasure trove of Greek myths to explore and enjoy.

So, there you have it! From far-flung invaders to the legendary Homer, Greek mythology has been a melting pot of influences and ideas, much like a hearty Greek moussaka. And just as we continue to savor this delicious dish today, the tales of ancient Greece continue to engage and enthrall us, generation after generation.

Understanding Greek Mythology

Greek Mythology is a wondrous collection of tales and legends that the ancient Greeks spun together, creating a vivid world filled with gods, heroes, and the mysteries of their universe. Let's embark on an epic quest to unravel the heart and soul of these spellbinding stories that have captivated generations.

A captivating ensemble of stories that ancient Greeks believed in, revealing their ideas about gods, heroes, the origins of their world, and the rituals that defined their lives. While creating gods was quite a popular hobby among ancient civilizations, the Greeks took it up a notch by fashioning deities that looked and behaved just like humans. Talk about divine doppelgängers!

The Greek gods had it all: beauty, power, wisdom, and even humor. With their unique personalities, they interacted with mortals in various towns and cities—many of which still exist today. From Mount Ida in Crete, the place where Zeus grew up, to the city of Thebes, where the hero Hercules built his home. It was in the same city of Thebes that Aphrodite was said to have emerged. The exact location of this occurrence can still be identified today, near the island of Cythera. These mythical places are rich in history and intrigue.

Greek myths often revolved around the extraordinary deeds of divine beings, who assisted humans in overcoming obstacles and achieving great feats. Take, for example, the Trojan Horse, that ingenious creation of Ulysses that allowed Greek soldiers to infiltrate enemy territory in the most unexpected way. Who doesn't love a good sneak attack?

Although the roots of Greek Mythology stretch back to 2000 B.C., it wasn't until around 700 B.C. that things really started to heat up. Enter the poetic trifecta: Homer's "Iliad" and "Odyssey" and Hesiod's "Theogony." These classic works solidified the myths and beliefs of ancient Greeks, capturing the essence of their world in verse.

These poems have a collection of myths that Ancient Greeks believed in and lived by. Some of the commonly followed myths are the following. So grab your toga, dear reader, and let's dive into the mystical world of ancient Greece, where gods and mortals mingle, and where the impossible becomes reality!

Mount Olympus – The Home of Gods

You may have heard of Mount Olympus, the celestial abode of the Greek gods, but did you know it was established after a battle royal called the Titanomachy? The Olympians, a new generation of gods, duked it out with the Titans, their predecessors, and claimed Mount Olympus as their lofty prize.

The Greeks believed that the gods lived high above the clouds in a palace on Mount Olympus, enjoying divine views and throwing legendary parties. However, they weren't limited to staying put—they were free to roam the mortal world and stir things up!

Worshipping Beliefs

The ancient Greeks thought their gods kept an eye on them from above and occasionally meddled in their lives. If a god was in a bad mood, they could whip up a storm to wreak havoc on a city, or give their favorite mortal an unfair advantage in battle. To keep their deities appeased, the Greeks built temples and offered animal sacrifices.

Each city in Greece had a patron god or goddess to protect its people from harm. When in need, the locals would flock to the temples to pray and make offerings, ensuring their divine protector stayed on their good side.

Life After Death

The Greeks also believed in life after death, envisioning an underground realm called "The Underworld." They believed that the souls of the deceased had to cross the River Styx to reach their final destination. To do so, they had to pay Charon, a grumpy ferryman who wouldn't budge without a coin. The Greeks placed a coin in the mouths of the deceased, ensuring their loved ones could afford the fare.

Once in the Underworld, the souls faced judgment by three stern judges. Good souls enjoyed eternal bliss in the Elysian Fields, while the so-so ones spent their days in the Asphodel Meadows (not too shabby!). But for the truly wicked, eternal torment awaited in the dreaded pit of Tartarus.

With this overview of the Greeks and their mythology in mind, let's dive deeper into their fantastical world. Just as the Christian Bible starts with Genesis, Greek mythology has its own version of how the world came to be—so let's turn the page and explore the cosmic beginnings of their universe!

CHAPTER 2
Cosmogony

The Creation of the World

In the beginning, there was only chaos - a real mess! The elements that would form the universe were all there, but mixed in an indistinct mass of confusion. This era of primordial chaos lasted for quite a while. Then, from the chaos, Gaia, the mother earth, emerged, an extremely fertile goddess. Gaia brought our planet to life and created all the land that covers it, like a super caring mom.

She generated numerous primordial deities like Pontus, the God of the sea, and the Ourea, the deities of the mountains. Gaia also gave birth to the God Uranus, a supreme being who would personify the sky and rule over everything. Uranus married Gaia, and they began their life together among the clouds. Even Nyx, the goddess of night, emerged from the chaos. She spent her time wandering the sky, covering it with her black cloak, like some sort of night DJ.

Uranus and Gaia met every day at dusk, and the fruits of their union began to sprout quickly. Gaia gave birth to terrifying creatures, including the Hecatoncheires, monsters with 100 arms and many heads, and the Cyclopes, who were mighty beings with a single eye. Uranus and Gaia also generated a new generation of gods, powerful beings who would become known as the Titans.

However, Uranus wasn't exactly a loving father. Seeing the powerful offspring he had generated, he began to fear being dethroned. So, he decided to send all his children to Tartarus, a dark place deep within the earth - the worst punishment he could imagine. The Titans, trapped in Gaia's womb, violently struck the walls of Tartarus, trying to escape. Gaia suffered terribly from this.

So, Gaia decided to conspire against her husband. She asked one of her children to eliminate Uranus. All the Titans refused, except for Cronus, the most ambitious of all, who was convinced he could perform the task. Gaia gave him a diamond sickle, and Cronus headed for the sky with determination.

Cronus found Uranus asleep on a cloud, and with a swift blow of his sickle, castrated his father. Uranus' scream of pain was heard throughout the universe, and the sky turned red like Uranus' blood. Uranus' testicles were thrown into the ocean, and many deities emerged from the waters, thanks to his incredible fertility.

Cronus returned victorious and freed his imprisoned brothers, becoming the hero of the revolt and the new Supreme Lord of the universe. However, Cronus did not free the Hecatoncheires or the Cyclopes, fearing they were too dangerous. So, they remained in Tartarus. After celebrating the victory with a great feast, Cronus received a visit from the specter of his father, who revealed a terrible prophecy: he told him that just as he had dethroned his father, Cronus would also lose the throne at the hands of his son. So, karma would come back to bite him, and that would be his terrible fate.

The Origin of the Olympian Gods

Cronus, the cruel ruler of the universe, reigned supreme after dethroning his father Uranus and freeing the Titans. These powerful beings, siblings of Cronus, supported him in his dominion over the world and he had no rivals. However, Cronus was tormented by a curse invoked by his father, which stated that one of his children would overthrow him from power.

Cronus married the Titaness Rhea, a goddess loved and respected by all. When Rhea gave birth to their first child, Cronus' fear of being dethroned led him to reveal his darkest side. He devoured Hestia, the eldest, and continued to consume every newborn that Rhea handed over to him, despite the desperate cries and pleas of the mother.

Rhea was determined to save at least one of her children from Cronus' cruelty. When she became pregnant again, she devised a plan to hide the baby from her husband. Rhea took refuge in a cave on the island of Crete, far from Cronus' gaze, and there she gave birth to a beautiful child with incredible power. Rhea felt that the Fates had woven a glorious future for her child and named him Zeus. She entrusted the infant to the care of nymphs and the Corybantes, who muffled the baby's cries with the clanging of their shields. Meanwhile, Rhea deceived Cronus by bringing him a stone wrapped in a cloth instead of the newborn. Cronus swallowed the stone without hesitation, while the queen wept on her knees. This time, her tears were not of sadness, but of emotion for having saved her child's life.

On the island of Crete, Zeus grew up unbeknownst to Cronus, nourished by the milk of the goat Amalthea and becoming increasingly strong and powerful. As an adult, Zeus was unexpectedly visited by Metis, a wise deity, who revealed the terrible fate of his siblings imprisoned in the Titan's stomach and gave him a magical potion to free his brothers.

Zeus, in disguise, went to Mount Othrys, the fortress of the Titans, and presented himself before Cronus, offering him the potion as divine nectar. Cronus, feeling invincible and not believing that anyone would dare to conspire against him, accepted the gift and, unaware of the deception, drank the entire potion. Soon he began to feel nauseous and was forced to vomit his children, now adults and eager for revenge: Hestia, Hera, Demeter, Hades, and Poseidon. Cronus also vomited the stone he had swallowed by deception. This stone, the Omphalos Stone, still plays a starring role in the Sanctuary of Delphi. Thus, with his siblings at his side, Zeus led a rebellion that would forever change the destiny of the universe.

Titanomachy - The War Between Gods and Titans

After freeing his siblings from the stomach of the fearsome Titan Cronus, Zeus led them to the summit of Mount Olympus, the highest mountain in Greece. There, they would establish the headquarters of the rebel gods, ready to fight against the oppression of the titans.

This rebellion gave rise to the Titanomachy, better known as the war of the titans. From his throne on Mount Othrys, Cronus gathered his loyal titans for the great battle. The general of Cronus' army was the Titan Atlas, tasked with leading the attacks against the gods of Olympus.

The plains of Thessaly became the battlefield between the armies of the gods and the titans. Initially, the titans seemed to have the upper hand, thanks to their immense physical strength. But Zeus, cunning as he was, released the cyclopes, strange creatures with only one eye. In gratitude, they forged formidable weapons for the gods: Zeus received his famous and powerful lightning bolt; Poseidon received a majestic trident capable of creating earthquakes and tsunamis; and Hades, the helm of terror that granted him the power of invisibility.

Thanks to these new weapons, the gods managed to hold their ground against the gigantic titans. The battle between the gods and the titans lasted nearly 10 years, filled with intense combat and bloody confrontations. It seemed that fate still favored the titans until Zeus had a brilliant idea: to release the fearsome Hecatoncheires from Tartarus, giants with 100 arms and 50 heads!

These monstrous creatures had a decisive impact on the war. The titan army was gripped by panic when faced with these grotesque beings. Zeus then gathered all his strength to infuse even more power into his mighty lightning bolt. With a thunderbolt, Zeus struck the head of Cronus, shaking the entire universe.

The titans were defeated and severely punished. Cronus and his allies were sentenced to a life of imprisonment in Tartarus, with the Hecatoncheires standing guard. Zeus reserved a special punishment for the Titan Atlas, leader of the titan troops: he was condemned to bear the weight of the celestial sphere on his shoulders for all eternity.

The Olympian gods now reigned supreme, under the command of Zeus. A new order began in the universe, all thanks to an epic clash of cosmic proportions!

The Creation of Humanity - The Punishment of Prometheus

In the beginning of time, the Earth was ruled by the Titans, powerful deities who were the children of primordial gods. Among them was Prometheus, a god as ancient as time itself, gifted with prophetic abilities. This cunning Titan managed to foresee the victory of the Olympian gods over the Titans in the Titanomachy, the epic battle for supreme power. He escaped imprisonment in Tartarus along with a few other Titans, not opposing Zeus during the conflict.

With the war over and the Olympian gods in command, Zeus assigned Prometheus and his brother Epimetheus the task of creating and populating the Earth with animals of every kind. The Titans had plenty of raw materials, and while Epimetheus shaped each type of creature, Prometheus coordinated the production process. Each animal was given a talent: birds were given the ability to fly, elephants immense strength, and talents were distributed evenly. Man was saved for last, as they wanted to create something special. However, after shaping man from clay, they realized that all talents had already been assigned to the other animals.

Prometheus presented his work to the goddess Athena, who, marveling at the Titan's creation, decided to bless it with divine breath. And so humanity was born! But Prometheus was not entirely satisfied: man was merely a slightly more intelligent monkey. Man lived in caves, avoiding other animals, feeding on fallen fruit, and fearing the darkness.

Athena suggested that Prometheus give fire to man. At sunset, the Titan headed towards the chariot of Helios, which awaited a new dawn. Prometheus lit the torch that would be given to humanity. With fire, man began to progress rapidly: weapons and tools were created, and man began to dominate nature.

Prometheus was finally happy, as the benevolent creator of humanity. Watching this new creature flourish, Zeus decreed that humanity would honor the gods by offering sacrifices. But Prometheus interceded on behalf of humanity, preventing his creation from being exploited.

Prometheus was very cunning and tried to deceive Zeus on behalf of men. He asked that a bull be sacrificed to the gods. The product of the sacrifice would be divided into two piles: one was smaller but contained the best meat covered by the animal's skin; the other pile was larger but contained only bones and entrails, wrapped in fat, which made the offering appealing. The cunning Prometheus knew that Zeus's ambition would lead him to choose the larger pile, while man would get the better part, and he was right.

Realizing he had been deceived, Zeus became furious with those who had tricked him and decided to take fire away from humanity. Without fire, humanity began to regress. They were tormented again by darkness and cold, and they could no longer cook their food. Indignant, Prometheus decided to steal the sacred fire and return it to man. During the night, he went to Mount Olympus and returned with the flame stolen from Hephaestus's forges.

With the reestablishment of fire's dominion, humanity began to prosper again, but the glowing flames caught Zeus's attention at night. Furious, the supreme God decided that Prometheus could not go unpunished for his insolence. He imprisoned Prometheus on a rock in the Caucasus to endure eternal punishment for defying Zeus's decisions.

But Prometheus's punishment was not merely life imprisonment; his torment would be terrible: Zeus decided that a monstrous bird would be assigned to devour his liver, causing him immeasurable pain. Prometheus was an immortal Titan, so after being torn apart by the abominable bird, his liver regenerated, only to be attacked again by the creature the next day.

The Titan endured this punishment for many painful years. Then Zeus descended to Earth and offered him freedom if he hid the knowledge of fire from mankind. As the benefactor of humanity, Prometheus refused the offer of the God and chose to sacrifice himself for his creation. Thanks to this, humanity was able to prosper and continue to develop through the sacrifice of Prometheus. And so, posterity remembers him as a hero, who defied the gods for the good of humanity, giving us the gift of fire and, with it, the possibility of reaching heights never before imagined.

Pandora's Box

In the beginning of time, the Titan brothers Prometheus and Epimetheus were tasked with creating mankind. To help his creation thrive, Prometheus decided to steal the sacred fire from the gods and give it to humanity. The Titan knew he wouldn't go unpunished for such a bold act and that sooner or later, the gods would punish him. So, aware of the looming danger for his brother and humanity, Prometheus warned Epimetheus: "Dear brother, my misfortune may not be enough to appease Zeus's wrath. Remember, never accept any gifts from the gods. By doing so, you will protect our creation."

Epimetheus thanked Prometheus for the advice and promised not to accept any gifts from the gods. However, just as Prometheus had predicted, Zeus devised a plan to take revenge on Epimetheus and humanity. Zeus ordered Hephaestus to create the first woman, the beautiful Pandora. The gods bestowed numerous gifts upon her, including unparalleled beauty from Aphrodite, the gift of speech from Hermes, and the Charites adorned her with clothes and jewelry.

Zeus sent Hermes to offer Pandora as a gift to Epimetheus, but not before giving her a mysterious box with a warning: "Bring this gift to mankind, but never open it for any reason." Epimetheus was so captivated by Pandora's breathtaking beauty that he forgot his brother's advice and accepted the gift.

Once at Epimetheus's home, Pandora couldn't contain her curiosity about the contents of the box. "What harm could a little peek do?" she thought innocently. So she opened the box, a powerful force pushed Pandora away, and a dark mist began to emerge from the box, releasing all the evils that Prometheus had avoided creating in humans. Until that moment, humanity had lived in the golden age, free from suffering and conflict, in a world of pure happiness. But now, thanks to Pandora's impulsive act, envy, cruelty, greed, illness, and hunger spread among humans.

Pandora desperately tried to close the box, but it was too late. Every evil had already escaped, but at the bottom of the box, hope still remained. And so, despite adversity, hope continued to give humanity the strength to face obstacles and difficulties in life. And Zeus, that old trickster, managed to prolong the punishment inflicted on mankind because, as we all know, hope is the last thing to die!

Gigantomachy

Gaia, the mother earth, still harbored a strong resentment towards the gods of Olympus. They had imprisoned her children, the titans, in the dark depths of Tartarus. To take revenge, Gaia fertilized the blood spilled by Uranus during his beheading, giving birth to a lineage of strong and powerful giants.

These 24 colossi had only one goal: to dethrone the gods of Mount Olympus. The gods, however, were not willing to be defeated and joined forces to face their formidable enemies in a fight to defend the new cosmic order and prevent a return to chaos.

And so begins the Gigantomachy, an epic struggle between the gods and the giants. But, oh dear, the gods seemed to be in trouble! Even their most powerful blows could not defeat the giants. It was then that Hera, the queen of the gods, revealed with great displeasure a prophecy: the gods could only win with the help of a powerful mortal dressed in a lion's skin. There was only one man on earth who fit this description: his name was Hercules. Zeus then instructed Athena to find Hercules and have him join the gods' battle. In the meantime, the giants, rooted in the earth in which they were born, near Thrace, began to gather huge stones in an attempt to reach the heavenly abode of the gods.

They were intent on protecting their building, the beating heart of their hopes, when a terrifying roar froze them in place. They didn't have the time to think, nor the courage to investigate: they fled at full speed, never looking back. But what they didn't know was that the terrible roar was only the braying of Silenus' donkey, the faithful companion leading his pupil Dionysus into battle. Silenus, drunk as always, showed no fear. With the confidence of a hero and the sly demeanor of a drunkard, he chased after the giants, riding his donkey, who advanced with the majesty of a proud steed. The realization of the deception struck the giants like a punch in the stomach, but it was already too late. They regrouped, charging back with renewed fury, but Silenus had already bought the necessary time. And here came Hercules, his bow drawn to the limit, he fired one of his arrows with unimaginable power, hitting a giant squarely. But there was a problem: when the giant fell, the ground seemed to awaken him, giving him new life. The gods understood that the giants had to be taken far from their homeland to be defeated. Hercules, with his legendary strength, accomplished the feat. He grabbed a giant and dragged him into unknown territory, where the earth could no longer restore his life. There, with his trusted club, he finally brought him down. The formidable giant Porphyrion dared to challenge the venerable goddess Hera, but was struck full-force by a love dart from Eros. Even under the effect of this wound, his aggression did not subside; on the contrary, it transformed into a lustful desire. Zeus watched this relentless attack with mounting jealousy until he decided to intervene. He unleashed one of his most formidable thunderbolts, striking the giant with divine energy. Meanwhile, Ares, the formidable god of war, was courageously battling against the horde of giants. However, despite being a skilled warrior, he found himself on his knees, overwhelmed by the superior forces of the enemy. It was at this critical juncture that Apollo and Hercules came to his rescue. With their sharp arrows, keen as a scythe, they managed to fell another one of the giants. Gradually, the gods confronted and weakened the insurrection of the giants, paving the way for Hercules who, with his legendary strength, delivered the final blow. One after another, the giants toppled, falling defeated. Dionysus crushed the giants with his thyrsus, while Hecate incinerated them with her fiery torches. Athena, with a clever move, hurled a huge boulder at the giant

Enceladus, who tried to escape across the sea. That gigantic boulder became the island of Sicily, located in the Italian peninsula.

Even Hades, the lord of the underworld, participated in the battle by wielding his pitchfork and lending Hermes his helmet of invisibility. Hermes, made invisible by the magical helmet, ran among the giants delivering lethal blows with his caduceus. Finally, Zeus triumphed, driving his chariot over the bodies of the fallen giants, having at his side Nike, the goddess of victory. The valiant Hercules was rewarded with great honors and tributes. Without him, the giants would have surely plunged the universe into chaos. And so, thanks to the daring and courage of the gods and heroes, order was maintained and the Gigantomachy went down in history as one of the greatest battles ever fought.

The Universal Flood

Once upon a time, the men created by Prometheus and his brother lived happily in the world. It was the golden age of mankind, when happiness flowed like rivers and everything was smooth sailing. But, unfortunately, those good times were long gone. Men, endowed with talents that distinguished them from other animals, ended up challenging the power of nature, transforming themselves into corrupt and evil creatures. Greed took over, and peace seemed to have vanished forever from the face of the Earth. Zeus, the king of the gods, was furious! He decided to take drastic measures and summoned Poseidon, the god of the sea, to Mount Olympus. With a stern and indignant expression, Zeus ordered his brother to flood the planet to exterminate all men. Poseidon, not wanting to contradict his brother, plunged his trident into the ground, causing huge cracks from which powerful jets of water gushed.

The world was submerged in the blink of an eye. Millions of men lost their lives in the raging waves of Poseidon. Ships were overturned and destroyed by the fury of the ocean. The gods of Olympus, astonished, watched the devastation caused by Zeus's wrath. Worried, they wondered what the world would be like without men. After all, who would worship the gods, if not them?

Thanks to the wisdom of Athena, Zeus transformed the end of the human race into a new beginning. He spared Deucalion, son of Prometheus, and Pyrrha, daughter of Epimetheus and Pandora. They were the best among humans, respectful and fearful of the gods, and managed to survive the flood on a small boat. When the waters receded, the world was unrecognizable, devastated, and desolate. Deucalion and Pyrrha searched through the ruins of many cities but found no trace of human life. They decided to visit the temple of the goddess Themis, the goddess of justice, hoping to receive an answer on how to repopulate the world. The couple prayed intensely, and the temple statue cryptically responded: "To repopulate the Earth, put the bones of your grandmother on your shoulders. In this way, humanity will live again." Pyrrha was perplexed: why would a goddess ask for such a dishonorable gesture towards her grandmother's tomb?

Deucalion, however, understood the hidden message. He consoled his wife and explained that the statue referred to the grandmother of all beings, Gaia, the goddess of the earth. Those "bones" were, in fact, the stones that made up the earth's surface. So, the couple got to work and began collecting stones, placing them on their shoulders. Each time a stone fell to the ground, a figure of a man emerged, which then transformed into a real person. The stones thrown by Deucalion gave life to men, while those thrown by Pyrrha generated women.

As Deucalion and Pyrrha wandered the world, they sowed new men and women, repopulating the Earth. And as the world slowly came back to life, the gods of Olympus smiled, reassured to see that their great experiment - humanity - had been given a second chance. And so, thanks to the wisdom of the gods and the faith of Deucalion and Pyrrha, the Earth was repopulated, and the Universal Flood went down in history as a warning to humanity: a reminder of the importance of respecting and venerating the gods, and how dangerous it can be when greed and corruption take over. And, of course, every time it rained a little more than usual, people looked around with a nervous smile, hoping that Zeus had not decided to repeat the experiment!

CHAPTER 3

Olympus and the Greek gods

The Gods

Zeus

Zeus, the most famous and larger-than-life of the Olympic Gods. As king of the gods, he ruled the sky like a celestial maestro, commanding the weather with the flick of his wrist. When Zeus was in a foul mood, watch out! He'd hurl lightning bolts and unleash booming storms from his penthouse suite on Mount Olympus. But Zeus was more than just a thunderous weather god with a temper; his personality was as vast as the sky he ruled.

This mighty deity was known for his leadership and wisdom. As king, he played referee to the other gods, making sure they didn't wreak too much havoc on the mortals below. He was the ultimate judge, settling disputes among gods and humans with his all-knowing sense of justice. Zeus was also a bit of a superhero, defending those who sought his help, especially against injustice and tyranny.

Now, let's talk about Zeus' mischievous side, which often landed him in some steamy situations. He was a notorious flirt, never hesitating to pursue mortal women and goddesses alike. This wandering eye led to a whole bunch of wild escapades, resulting in countless children—gods, demi-gods, you name it. Some of his most famous offspring include

Hercules, Perseus, and Helen of Troy. Talk about a family tree!

Despite his, ahem, extracurricular activities, Zeus was a devoted husband to his sister-wife, Hera, the queen of the gods. Their relationship was like a Greek soap opera—filled with jealousy, revenge, and passion. But in the end, love always conquered, and they found their way back to each other.

Zeus' insatiable curiosity and love for disguises made for some thrilling adventures. He often took on different forms, such as animals or even humans, to mingle with the mortals. These escapades not only fed his curiosity but also helped him better understand the human experience. Talk about going undercover!

In a nutshell, Zeus was a complex character who embodied power, wisdom, and a dash of mischief. As the ruler of the gods, he was both a protector and a philanderer, always taking center stage in the enchanting world of Greek mythology.

Apollo

Apollo, the dazzling runner-up in the "Most Important Greek God" pageant, was in charge of the celestial light show as the god of the sun. He not only provided warmth during the day, but also ensured the perfect conditions for sowing crops. However, Apollo was more than just your run-of-the-mill sun god; he was also the epitome of handsomeness, masculinity, and an impressive array of talents that made him stand out among his divine squad.

Apollo was quite the enigma, blending Greek and non-Greek elements in his divine persona. As an advocate of moderation, he appeared to embody a harmonious balance between two distinct flavors. This unique combo made him an interesting character on the Greek mythology menu.

One slice of Apollo could be traced back to Near Eastern sun gods, who were typically appeased with all-you-can-offer sacrifices. In some regions, this sun god might have even outshined Zeus or the local equivalent. It's important to remember that Greek mythology is like a divine buffet, with a melting pot of various local belief systems. Apollo symbolized the fusion of different gods, creating a deity who was a sun god with a side of something extra.

While there may have been something non-Greek about Apollo, his aesthetic and qualities were Greek. Greek society was highly patriarchal, much like Rome, and the emphasis on male beauty and power being two sides of the same coin seems to be a natural extension of this androcentrism.

Apollo's characteristics didn't just stop at his sun-kissed looks and radiant job. He was also the god of music, arts, and poetry, often depicted with a lyre in hand. As a patron of the arts, he inspired creativity and artistic expression in both gods and mortals like a divine muse.

Moreover, Apollo was a skilled archer and held the title of the god of healing and medicine. He had the power to both cause and cure diseases, making him a deity who could give life with one hand and take it away with the other. His twin sister, Artemis, shared his expertise in archery, and the two were known as a formidable tag team.

Last but not least, Apollo moonlighted as the god of prophecy and truth, having established the famous Oracle of Delphi. His divine foresight allowed him to guide mortals and gods alike, offering wisdom and advice for those who sought it like a celestial fortune teller.

Apollo was a multifaceted god who exemplified a harmonious blend of diverse elements. As the god of the sun, music, arts, healing, and prophecy, he held a prominent position in Greek mythology. Apollo's unique characteristics made him a captivating and influential figure, combining power and beauty in the ancient world like a divine Greek salad.

Hermes

Hermes, the speedy messenger of the Greek gods, was a jack-of-all-trades and a multitasking marvel. With his swift feet, he zipped between the realms of mortal men and ageless gods faster than you could say "hermeneutics." He quickly became the go-to deity for travelers and traders, who appreciated his expediency and resourcefulness.

But Hermes wasn't just known for his speedy deliveries; he was also a bit of a rascal. As the god of thieves, his penchant for trickery and silver-tongued oration made him a popular choice for those who occasionally needed to bend the truth or "borrow" something without asking.

Hermes wasn't one to shy away from crossing boundaries, whether between the human and divine realms or between the world of the living and the dead. He played a crucial role in escorting the souls of the deceased to the underworld, where he handed them off to Charon for a safe and timely passage. As the god of the road and sports, Hermes had fans ranging from everyday folks to elite athletes in ancient Greece.

With a versatile nature and a diverse set of talents, Hermes starred in countless adventures and stories. One of his most famous escapades involved helping Zeus eliminate Argus, allowing Zeus to continue his rather scandalous relationship with Io. In another tale, Zeus asked Hermes to create an eternal wheel of spinning fire for Ixion. Hermes was the kind of god who got things done, even if it meant getting his hands a little dirty.

During the Trojan War and Ulysses' epic journey home, Hermes played a pivotal role. While he supported the Greeks in their battle against the Trojans, his unpredictable nature allowed him to protect Trojan King Priam as he sneaked into the Greek camp to retrieve his slain son Hector. Hermes' trickster skills were passed down to the cunning hero Ulysses, as Hermes' great-grandson. The Greeks prayed to Hermes while devising their famous Trojan Horse plan, and with his divine assistance, they pulled off the ultimate Trojan takedown.

Hermes was a god of many talents and characteristics. As the messenger of the gods, protector of travelers, god of thieves, and guide to the underworld, he held a prominent position in Greek mythology. His swift feet and cunning nature made him a valuable ally and a captivating figure in the thrilling world of ancient Greece—and, frankly, someone you'd want on your team during trivia night.

Hades

Hades, the god of the underworld, wasn't exactly the life of the party in ancient Greece. As one of the three top-dog Olympian brothers—along with Zeus and Poseidon—Hades ruled the underworld with a unique flair that put him in a league of his own.

While Zeus hogged the limelight with his thunderbolts and majestic sky, and Poseidon made waves with his control of the sea, Hades forged his own distinct path as the underworld's top dog. Sure, it wasn't as flashy as his brothers' gigs, but Hades brought his own brand of cool to the table.

Born as the first Olympian, Hades had the rather unfortunate experience of being swallowed by his dad, Cronus. Luckily, when Zeus forced dear old dad to cough up his siblings, Hades emerged last, now the youngest of the bunch!

During the epic Olympian gods vs. Titans showdown, Hades proved to be a force to be reckoned with, helping Zeus snatch the throne. And although some ancient tales suggest Hades was initially bummed about his underworld assignment, he quickly grew into his new role, ruling with an iron fist and keeping the dearly departed on their toes, regardless of their VIP status.

But don't let Hades' tough exterior fool you—there was more to him than just his stern demeanor and unyielding authority. He had a strong sense of justice, ensuring that souls in the underworld received a fair shake based on their life choices. This made him quite the respected figure among mortals and gods alike.

When it came to matters of the heart, Hades was head over heels for his wife, Persephone, the goddess of spring and fertility. Their love story had its share of drama (kidnapping, anyone?), but ultimately showcased a softer side of the underworld's kingpin.

And let's not forget, Hades was also the godfather of wealth. With the underworld being the source of precious metals and gems, he was sometimes known as "Pluton" or "the rich one." Talk about a figure with hidden treasures!

Hades was a multifaceted god who brought his own brand of cool to the underworld. As the ruler of life and death, justice, loyalty, and wealth, he was a captivating and essential figure in the world of Greek mythology. So next time you think of Hades, remember: he wasn't just the god of the underworld—he was the life and soul of it, too!

Poseidon

Let's dive into the world of Poseidon, the mighty Greek sea god who had a special place in the hearts of seafaring Greeks. As the protector of sea creatures and those who traveled by sea, Poseidon was a real star among fishermen and sailors. Given the Greeks' love affair with the ocean, it's no wonder that Poseidon made quite the splash as a powerful and essential deity.

Now, as king of the sea, Poseidon had a few tricks up his sleeve—or should we say, tucked beneath his waves? His weapon of choice was the trident, a fearsome three-pronged staff that he wielded with great power. You might say he had a point or three to make. In art and sculpture, Poseidon often posed with this iconic symbol, asserting his watery authority.

Let's not forget Poseidon's fabulous fashion statement: a distinctive crown adorned with sea-related elements like seashells and conchs. This majestic accessory served as a reminder that when it came to the ocean and its creatures, Poseidon was the big fish in charge.

Speaking of creatures, Poseidon had quite the entourage. He ruled over an enchanting array of aquatic beings, including nymphs and nereids. These humanoid sea and water creatures were the life of the underwater party, and their presence in Greek mythology showcased the culture's fascination with personifications of bodies of water. This sea-centric focus was a uniquely Greek characteristic, making Poseidon the talk of the pantheon.

As a god, Poseidon had a temper that could rival the fiercest storm. With his moody disposition, he could whip up violent storms, earthquakes, and other calamities when enraged. But fear not! When Poseidon was in a good mood, he would grant safe passage to sailors and bountiful catches to fishermen. It just goes to show, it's always a good idea to stay on a sea god's good side.

Aside from his role as the sea god, Poseidon had a hidden talent: he was also a horse whisperer. As the "Earth-Shaker," he held dominion over horses and was believed to have created the first one. Naturally, he became associated with horsemanship and equestrian activities.

Poseidon's fan base extended far and wide, with worshipers in Greek cities like Marathon near Athens and Paestum in Southern Italy. His influence knew no bounds, proving his significance in Greek mythology.

Poseidon was a multifaceted god who embodied the power and unpredictability of the sea. With his trusty trident and crown of seashells, he ruled over a fascinating realm of sea creatures and watery wonders. As the protector of sailors, fishermen, and horses, Poseidon made waves as a vital and captivating figure in the world of Greek mythology.

Ares

Ares, the Greek god of war, might seem like the unsung hero of mythology, often playing second fiddle to other gods in wartime. But don't be fooled! There's more to this underdog than meets the eye. Let's face it, everybody loves a good supporting character.

As the god of war, Ares was notorious for his hot temper and love of violence. His fearlessness and insatiable bloodlust made him a force to be reckoned with on the battlefield, sending chills down the spines of mortals and gods alike. Sure, he may not have been the go-to choice for divine intervention, but you've got to admit, the guy had style.

When it comes to family drama, Ares could give any reality TV show a run for its money. His torrid love affair with Aphrodite, the goddess of love and beauty, was the talk of Mount Olympus. The two shared a passionate, if not tumultuous, relationship that left Aphrodite's husband, Hephaestus, steaming with jealousy. This divine love triangle was more than just juicy gossip; it highlighted the very human aspect of infidelity. Ares certainly knew how to stir the pot, both on and off the battlefield.

Though Ares wasn't the most popular kid on the block, he did have a loyal following in a few Ancient Greek cities, like Sparta, where his warrior spirit was highly valued. And let's not forget his Roman alter ego, Mars, who enjoyed a much more prestigious status and even fathered the legendary founders of Rome, Romulus and Remus.

Ares wasn't just about war and scandal; he also represented courage, strength, and the raw energy of youth. Often depicted as a strapping young man, he was the embodiment of vigor and vitality. His symbols, like the spear, shield, and helmet, further emphasized his warrior persona.

In the grand scheme of Greek mythology, Ares might have been overshadowed by other gods and goddesses, but his unique characteristics made him stand out in his own right. As the god of war, he personified fearlessness, bloodlust, and untamed energy. His steamy love affair with Aphrodite added an extra layer of intrigue to his story, making him a captivating figure. So, while Ares may not have been the star of the show, he still played a memorable part in the epic drama that was Greek mythology. Break a leg, Ares!

Hephaestus

Hephaestus, the divine blacksmith of the gods and hubby to the stunning Aphrodite, might strike you as the odd one out in the glamorous world of Greek mythology. But let's be honest, who doesn't have a soft spot for the quirky underdog? In a lineup of chiseled and idealized gods, Hephaestus stood out with his down-to-earth appearance and refreshingly relatable nature.

As the god of fire, metalworking, and craftsmanship, Hephaestus knew a thing or two about working with his hands. He was the go-to guy for the gods' arsenal of powerful weapons, armor, and other divine knick-knacks. This skilled artisan could whip up anything from Zeus's thunderbolts to Helios's golden chariot. Now that's what we call a versatile resume!

Among the Olympians, Hephaestus wasn't exactly the poster child for beauty. While other gods were busy flaunting their youthful good looks, Hephaestus was often depicted as a rather unpretentious man. Legend has it that he was lame and walked with a limp, all thanks to being unceremoniously thrown off Mount Olympus by his own mother, Hera, who wasn't too thrilled with his less-than-perfect appearances. But Hephaestus didn't let that get him down; he embraced his uniqueness and poured his heart and soul into his work. After all, beauty is only skin deep, right?

Though he might seem like a bit player in Greek mythology, Hephaestus actually had his fair share of moments in the limelight. He played a part in the tale of King Minos and the Minotaur, crafting the bronze giant

Talos to safeguard Crete. He also showed up in the story of Jason and the Argonauts, forging the magical ship Argo. And let's not forget his rollercoaster marriage to Aphrodite, which often landed him front and center in stories of her steamy exploits and misadventures.

While Hephaestus might not have been the patron deity of many major cities, folks still knew how to show some love for the god of the forge. Shrines dedicated to him were a common sight, because who wouldn't want to pay their respects to the divine craftsman behind some of the most jaw-dropping creations in Greek mythology?

Hephaestus's unique characteristics made him a fascinating figure in the pantheon of Greek gods. As the divine blacksmith, he was the embodiment of creativity, skill, and perseverance. His less-than-perfect appearance and relatable challenges added depth to his character, making him a lovable and captivating figure. So, while Hephaestus might not have been the flashiest of the gods, he sure knew how to steal the show with his undeniable flair for the dramatic in the mesmerizing world of Greek mythology.

Dionysus

Dionysus, the god of wine, festivities, and all things merry, was the life of the party in the world of Greek mythology. Hailing from exotic Thracian origins, he brought a unique and intoxicating flair to the Greek pantheon. As the son of Zeus and a mortal mother, Dionysus was a fascinating blend of divine and mortal qualities, making him all the more irresistible.

Our dear Dionysus, as the god of wine, had quite the refined palate when it came to vineyards and winemaking. He was a key figure in Greek culture and Mediterranean life, where viticulture was as essential as a good bottle of red at a dinner party. Dionysus was always ready to spread joy and help even the most uptight mortals let their hair down.

No one could throw a party like Dionysus, who presided over the wild and raucous Bacchanalian festivals, named after his Latin alter ego, Bacchus. These hedonistic shindigs were far from your average soiree; think less potluck and more full-blown orgies that were believed to influence the wine harvest. The Greeks sure knew how to have a good time, and Dionysus was their main man for cutting loose.

In art and imagery, Dionysus often appeared as a bearded man clutching a cup of wine or a thyrsus (a staff topped with a pinecone, not a party hat). His entourage included a motley crew of rowdy revelers, such as satyrs, maenads, and other mythical party creatures. Dionysus had a knack for inspiring ecstasy and madness in his followers, making his parties a delightful mix of pleasure and pandemonium.

Beyond his role as the god of wine and festivities, Dionysus also dabbled in theater and the arts. As a patron of creativity and self-expression, he encouraged the Greeks to let their artistic freak flags fly and push the limits of their imagination. In this way, Dionysus championed both the physical and emotional aspects of human experience.

In most Greek cities, including Eleusis near Athens, Dionysus was celebrated with worship and wild parties. His presence could be felt at crossroads and in statues depicting a bearded man with a rather prominent phallus, serving as a cheeky reminder of his influence on Greek life.

Dionysus's characteristics made him a magnetic figure in Greek mythology. As the god of wine, festivities, and the arts, he embodied the spirit of revelry, creativity, and indulgence. His exotic origins and captivating mix of divine and mortal traits only added to his charm, making him a standout in the pantheon of Greek gods. So, let's raise a glass to Dionysus, the ultimate party god and the supreme symbol of life's pleasures and excesses. Cheers!

Goddesses

Hera

Hera, the queen of the gods and Zeus' wife, was a key player in Greek mythology. As the goddess of marriage and women, she showcased the best and worst of femininity with her unique blend of strength and vulnerability. With a healthy dose of irony in her story, Hera became a complex and enthralling character in the pantheon of Greek gods.

Despite her status as the goddess of marriage and women, Hera found herself powerless to stop her husband's philandering ways. Zeus' dalliances with mortals and other divine beings were a constant reminder that even the goddess of marriage couldn't keep her own relationship sacred. This continuous heartache led to a love-hate dynamic, where simmering rage bubbled beneath the surface, ready to erupt at any moment.

Hera's loyalty to Zeus was equal parts admirable and tragic. In spite of his countless infidelities, she still loved and supported him. But her heartache often transformed into a vengeful wrath, aimed at her husband's illegitimate offspring and their mothers. This dark side of Hera showed the depth of her pain and the extent of her betrayal.

One of the most famous examples of Hera's wrath was her animosity toward Hercules. This muscle-bound demigod was the son of Zeus and a mortal woman named Alcmene. Driven by her desire to erase any trace of her husband's infidelity, Hera tried to end Alcmene's pregnancy. But when Alcmene's clever servant, Galanthis, duped Hera into thinking the baby had already been born, Hera went into a fit of rage, transforming

Galanthis into a weasel. While Hercules may have dodged a bullet (or a lightning bolt) for the time being, Hera's grudge against him would last a lifetime.

But there's more to Hera than just her rocky marriage with Zeus. As the goddess of marriage and women, she stood as a powerful symbol of feminine authority and stability in ancient Greek society. Often depicted as a regal and dignified figure adorned with a crown and scepter, Hera exuded an air of authority. She was also closely associated with the peacock, a creature known for its beauty and grandeur, reflecting her own majestic presence.

Hera was a goddess of many contradictions: loving yet vengeful, loyal yet betrayed, and powerful yet vulnerable. These complex traits made her a fascinating figure in Greek mythology, revealing the multifaceted nature of femininity and the emotional rollercoaster that comes with love and betrayal. Through Hera's story, we're reminded of the incredible strength and resilience of women, even in the face of unimaginable heartache. So here's to Hera, a goddess whose story is as captivating as it is relatable.

Demeter

Demeter, the goddess of the harvest, has a special spot reserved in the Greek mythology hall of fame. Known as Mother Nature, she's the ultimate caretaker of Earth, making sure it provides nourishment for all living beings. Demeter's characteristics paint her as a symbol of life, abundance, and the ever-changing dance of the seasons.

As the goddess of the harvest, Demeter takes on the role of agricultural guru, teaching humans the tricks of the trade when it comes to farming. She handed down the knowledge they needed to grow corn and other essential crops. Thanks to Demeter's green thumb, people in ancient Greece were able to cultivate the land, feed their families, and—well—party like it was 480 BC.

Demeter's tender, motherly nature shines in her relationship with her daughter Persephone, who found herself abducted by Hades and whisked off to the underworld. With Persephone gone, Demeter became the poster goddess for heartache, neglecting her duties and plunging the Earth into a cold, barren state for half the year. Winter in Greece? Not the best time for a vacation.

But as soon as Persephone returns to her mom, Demeter's joy breathes life back into the Earth, kickstarting a beautiful renewal. This period represents the spring and summer months when crops thrive and life is in full swing. Thanks to Demeter, we get to witness nature's amazing ability to bounce back.

Demeter's fierce love for her daughter showcases her protective instincts.

She went to great lengths to find Persephone, striking a deal with Hades that let her daughter spend half the year with her mom and the other half in the underworld. Talk about a strong, resilient mama bear!

In art and mythology, Demeter often appears as a motherly figure, wearing a wreath of grain or holding sheaves of wheat. These symbols represent her connection to the harvest and the Earth. Sometimes, she's shown with a torch (flashlight not yet invented), signifying her search for her lost daughter, or surrounded by plants and animals, emphasizing her nurturing side.

Demeter's characteristics make her a pivotal figure in Greek mythology. As the goddess of the harvest and Mother Nature, she's the life force behind Earth's ever-changing seasons. Her love for Persephone and her unwavering devotion to her responsibilities reveal a goddess with a heart full of strength, tenderness, and resilience. Through Demeter's story, we learn about the power of love, the beauty of renewal, and the fact that everything in nature is connected—even in ancient Greece, it was a small world after all.

Aphrodite

Aphrodite, the goddess of beauty and love, is nothing short of a showstopper in Greek mythology. With her jaw-dropping looks and irresistible charm, she personifies passion, desire, and sensuality. Aphrodite's characteristics make her a fascinating and multi-faceted goddess whose allure knows no borders, playing a starring role in countless myths and legends.

Legend has it that Aphrodite was born from the ocean's foam when blood droplets from the defeated Titan, Uranus, splashed into the water. Her beauty was so stunning that even the gods on Mount Olympus feared an all-out divine war for her affections. Crafty Zeus, always looking out for number one, decided to nip this potential conflict in the bud by arranging for Aphrodite to marry Hephaestus, the least attractive god on the block. This unlikely pairing of beauty and, well, not-so-beauty was seen as a sort of cosmic balance, keeping the peace on Olympus.

Interestingly enough, Aphrodite wasn't your typical homegrown Greek goddess. Her worship in Greece came about through trade and cultural exchanges with the Near East. Picture ancient Greek merchants rubbing shoulders with the locals in places like Phoenicia and Syria, where they encountered sensual goddesses like Astarte. It wasn't long before Aphrodite made her grand entrance into Greek religion.

Despite being a foreign import, Aphrodite quickly became a central figure in numerous Greek myths. Whenever there was a whiff of love, passion, or desire in the air, Aphrodite was never far behind. Her beauty was the talk of both gods and mortals, and she even played a crucial role in the

Trojan War when Paris declared her the fairest of all with that infamous golden apple.

You've probably seen Aphrodite's iconic image: emerging from the sea, naked and standing on a seashell—a scene immortalized by Renaissance artist Botticelli. This portrayal captures her divine beauty and connection to the ocean, which gave birth to her astonishing presence.

As the patroness of Cnidus in Asia Minor and Paphos on Cyprus, Aphrodite enjoyed widespread worship and adoration. The Romans even knew her as Venus, further testament to her cross-cultural appeal.

Aphrodite's characteristics paint her as an enchanting and complex goddess. As the embodiment of beauty and love, she captured the hearts and desires of gods and mortals alike. Her intriguing origin story and widespread worship showcase her magnetic appeal, transcending cultural boundaries and securing her place as one of the most captivating figures in Greek mythology. Through Aphrodite's story, we glimpse the power of love and desire, as well as the undeniable allure of beauty that keeps us hooked to this day. And let's be honest, who can resist a goddess who knows how to make an entrance?

Eris

Eris, the goddess of strife and discord, is quite the troublemaker in Greek mythology. With her mischievous and chaotic nature, she loves to stir the pot, causing conflict and disharmony wherever she goes. Eris's characteristics reveal a complex and cunning goddess, whose antics could make you chuckle or shudder, depending on the situation.

As the goddess of strife and discord, Eris has a knack for causing trouble and instigating conflict. She's like that one friend who always seems to know the juiciest gossip and can't help but share it, even if it's just a little exaggerated. Whether through whispered rumors, subtle manipulations, or straight-up chaos, Eris's influence can be felt wherever drama and tension arise.

In the infamous story of the golden apple, Eris plays the role of the ultimate wedding crasher. Feeling snubbed by not being invited to a divine wedding, she decides to stir up some trouble by tossing a golden apple with the words "To the Fairest" inscribed on it among the goddesses Aphrodite, Hera, and Athena. Her sneaky plan works like a charm, and soon the goddesses are quarreling over who gets the title of "fairest."

Zeus, not wanting to get in the middle of this divine catfight, passes the buck to the mortal prince Paris, asking him to choose the fairest goddess. Each goddess, eager to win Paris's favor, offers him an enticing reward. In the end, it's Aphrodite's promise to help Paris marry the most beautiful woman on Earth, Helen, that wins him over. Unfortunately, Helen is already married, and her abduction by Paris leads to the devastating Trojan War. All this chaos and conflict, thanks to Eris's love for drama.

Eris is often depicted as a dark and sinister figure, symbolizing the destructive nature of conflict and discord. She's sometimes portrayed holding a torch or a whip, like some kind of chaos dominatrix. In some myths, Eris is described as the sister of Ares, the god of war, further cementing her connection to conflict and battle.

Eris's characteristics make her a fascinating and somewhat terrifying figure in Greek mythology. As the goddess of strife and discord, she serves as a reminder of the destructive power of conflict and the importance of harmony in both human and divine relationships. Eris's cunning nature and her ability to stir up trouble serve as a cautionary tale, reminding us that one person's mischief can lead to a whole lot of chaos. So the next time you feel like stirring the pot, just remember the story of Eris and think twice!

Athena

Athena, the goddess of war and wisdom, is a fascinating figure in Greek mythology. With a unique blend of brains and brawn, she's like the ultimate superhero of the ancient world. Athena's characteristics reveal a multifaceted goddess whose influence stretches far beyond the realms of war and learning.

As the goddess of war, Athena represents strategic thinking and the ability to keep her cool under pressure. Unlike her hotheaded brother Ares, who's all about the brute force of warfare, Athena prefers to outsmart her enemies with careful planning and cunning strategy. No wonder she's the go-to goddess for both mortals and gods in need of a little tactical advice.

But Athena's awesomeness doesn't stop there. She's also the goddess of wisdom, setting her apart from the rest of the Greek pantheon. Her intellectual prowess makes her the divine patron of learning, knowledge, and the arts. So, whether you're a poet, philosopher, or craftsman, Athena's got your back.

Now, let's talk about Athena's mind-blowing origin story. She wasn't just born; she burst forth fully formed and armored from Zeus's head! Talk about a headache. This extraordinary birth won her a special place in Zeus's heart, making her the apple of his divine eye.

Athena played a starring role in many Greek myths, including the story of Perseus and Medusa, where she acted as the hero's wise mentor. In art and mythology, she's often depicted wearing a helmet and carrying a spear, or dressed in full armor, showing off her warrior side. And let's not forget her trusty owl sidekick, symbolizing her wisdom and razor-sharp insight.

The city of Athens, named in her honor, held a special place in Athena's heart. As the city's protector and patron, she was revered and celebrated by its inhabitants. The Parthenon, a temple dedicated to Athena, stands as a testament to her importance in ancient Greek culture. And to the Romans, she was known as Minerva, proving that her influence knew no bounds.

Athena's characteristics make her a truly unique figure in Greek mythology. As the goddess of war and wisdom, she's a perfect blend of the fierce strength of a warrior and the sharp intellect of a scholar. Her role in various myths and her association with Athens have cemented her status as a beloved symbol of courage, wisdom, and strategic thinking. Athena's story serves as an inspiration for those seeking to balance knowledge and action, reminding us that true strength lies in the harmony of the mind and the heart. So, next time you're facing a challenge, channel your inner Athena and let the wisdom of the gods guide you!

Artemis

Artemis, the goddess of the hunt, the moon, and archery, is a fascinating character in Greek mythology. As the twin sister of Apollo and daughter of Zeus, she's got some serious divine street cred. Artemis's characteristics reveal a multifaceted and compassionate goddess, who served as a protector and nurturer of both people and animals in need.

Being the goddess of the hunt, Artemis was a skilled archer and a fierce huntress, deeply connected to the natural world. She roamed the wilderness with her entourage of nymphs and young girls, known as the Handmaidens of Artemis. Together, they hunted and shared in the sisterly camaraderie of their wild, untamed lives.

As the goddess of the moon, Artemis lit up the night sky guiding travelers on their journeys. This lunar connection made her a beacon of light and hope in the darkness. Artemis's presence was felt during the changing phases of the moon, reminding everyone that she was always keeping an eye on things.

One of Artemis's most defining characteristics was her role as a protector, particularly of young women and animals. She fiercely defended her charges against any threats, kind of like a divine big sister. Artemis's unwavering dedication to the vulnerable made her a fan-favorite among ancient Greeks.

In art and mythology, Artemis is often depicted as a beautiful woman dressed in hunting attire, armed with a bow and quiver of arrows. Her beauty was so legendary that it sparked the desire of mortal men like

Actaeon, who faced her wrath for daring to sneak a peek while she bathed.

Despite her vanity, which, let's be honest, was pretty standard among gods and goddesses, Artemis was revered for her unique attributes and qualities. Greek worship varied from region to region, with different groups focusing on specific divinities based on their needs and values. As a result, Artemis's fan club was deeply rooted in the regional character of the Greek world, including the Ionians, Dorians, and Aeolians.

Artemis's characteristics make her a truly unique and inspiring figure in Greek mythology. As the goddess of the hunt, the moon, and archery, she embodies strength, courage, and a deep connection to the natural world. Her role as a protector and nurturer has endeared her to countless generations, and her enduring influence continues to resonate in our modern world. Artemis's story reminds us of the importance of compassion and the power of a fiercely protective spirit, inspiring us to stand up for those who cannot defend themselves—just like a celestial superhero!

Hestia

Hestia, the Greek goddess of the hearth and fire, is quite the enigmatic character in Greek mythology. As the eldest daughter of Cronus and Rhea, she was not only Zeus's big sister but also the keeper of the home fires – literally! Hestia's unique characteristics reveal a goddess who embodies the cozy warmth, stability, and harmony of the home, while also offering a throwback to the good ol' days of ancient worship that came before the Achaeans and Dorians crashed the party.

As the goddess of the hearth, Hestia was the ultimate homebody. She made sure every home was warm, welcoming, and full of love. Her presence was felt in every household, where the hearth fire was the original hotspot for family gatherings. Hestia was the one you called upon during meals and get-togethers, ensuring everyone got their fair share of food, love, and laughter.

Hestia's fiery connection doesn't just stop at the hearth, though. She also provided the life-giving warmth that nurtured communities and kept everyone toasty. Thanks to Hestia, both individual households and society as a whole prospered and lived in harmony.

In a world where the other Olympians were all about drama and excitement, Hestia was a breath of fresh air. She was the peaceful, gentle goddess who preferred a cup of tea and a good book over petty squabbles and power struggles. Some scholars even think that the earliest Greek gods were more like Hestia – chill and peace-loving – and that the macho gods like Zeus and Apollo only came into the picture after some major cultural shake-ups.

Sure, this theory might be oversimplifying things a bit, but it does show just how influential Hestia was in Greek mythology. Her peaceful vibes and love for all things domestic remind us that a little balance and stability go a long way, both among gods and mere mortals.

In art and mythology, Hestia is often portrayed as a modestly dressed woman – no flashy outfits for this goddess! – sometimes holding a staff or a torch, symbols of her fiery passion for hearth and home. Unlike some of the other gods and goddesses, Hestia wasn't one for grand adventures or steamy love affairs; she was more of a behind-the-scenes kind of gal, offering comfort and support to those in need.

Hestia's characteristics make her a one-of-a-kind figure in Greek mythology. As the goddess of the hearth and fire, she's a warm reminder of the stability, harmony, and love that form the foundation of a thriving society. With her peaceful nature and unwavering dedication to the home and family, Hestia serves as a gentle reminder to appreciate the simpler things in life – like a crackling fire, a snug blanket, and the company of those we love. So, the next time you're gathered around the fireplace, take a moment to remember Hestia and the timeless values she represents.

Lesser Deities

Zeus, being the busy god he was, didn't just have children with Hera. He fathered quite a few lesser deities who, although they might not have been official Olympian gods, still had their own fan clubs and VIP spots on Mount Olympus. This diverse crowd included the Muses, Charites and Horai, Nymphs, Attis, Glaucus, and the ever-rambunctious Satyrs.

Often referred to as "nature-spirits," these divine beings were known for their love of the great outdoors. They could be found frolicking in the wilderness, splashing around in water, or taking leisurely strolls through the countryside. Some might say they were the original influencers, inspiring people to appreciate and connect with nature.

In many Greek rural cults, the female spirits, like nymphs and familiar presences, were quite the popular bunch. They brought a touch of magic to everyday life and had folks believing in the enchanting beauty of their surroundings. As for the male nature-spirits, they were more likely to be associated with literature and the arts. You might say they were the ancient world's muses, inspiring creativity and artistic expression.

So, while they might not have been top-tier Olympians, these lesser deities still had a significant impact on Greek culture and mythology. They added a little bit of whimsy and enchantment to the world, encouraging people to appreciate the natural beauty around them and to explore their creative sides. And let's be honest, who wouldn't want to hang out with a nature-loving spirit that could inspire your next masterpiece?

Muses

The Muses, affectionately known as "Mousai" in ancient Greece, were the fabulous goddesses of inspiration and creativity who lit up the hearts of poets, artists, and thinkers alike. These divine daughters of Zeus and Mnemosyne (the personification of memory, lest we forget!) each held a unique talent, working together like a well-oiled machine to inspire and support human creativity.

According to our dear friend Hesiod, the nine Muses were Euterpe, Melpomene, Erato, Thaleia, Kleio, Kalliope, Ourania, Polyhymnia, and Terpsichore. These lovely ladies specialized in different areas of the arts and sciences, making them the ultimate dream team for creative folks:

1. Euterpe: Known as the "Giver of Delight," Euterpe jazzed things up as the Muse of music and lyric poetry.

2. Melpomene: With her tragic mask and somber disposition, Melpomene was the go-to gal for tragedy and dramatic arts.

3. Erato: This Muse of love poetry and mimicry was a real heartbreaker with her passionate verses and performances.

4. Thaleia: As the Muse of comedy and light-hearted poetry, Thaleia kept the world laughing and having a good time.

5. Kleio: A true historian and patron of heroic poetry, Kleio made sure the stories of the past lived on for future generations.

6. Kalliope: Often considered the queen bee of the Muses, Kalliope inspired epic poetry and eloquence, guiding literary legends like Homer and Hesiod.

7. Ourania: With her eyes fixed on the heavens, Ourania was the Muse of astronomy and celestial knowledge.

8. Polyhymnia: The Muse of sacred hymns and meditation, Polyhymnia brought peace and introspection to spiritual seekers.

9. Terpsichore: As the Muse of dance and choral poetry, Terpsichore added rhythm and grace to the world's dance floors.

The Muses weren't shy about showing off their talents, either. There are a few myths about mortals bold enough to challenge their singing abilities—spoiler alert: the Muses usually won, proving their unmatched skills.

These characteristics make the Muses truly one-of-a-kind in Greek mythology. As the goddesses of inspiration, they embody the beauty, passion, and intellect that drive human creativity. Their influence touches every aspect of the arts and sciences, reminding us that inspiration is always just around the corner. By honoring the Muses, we celebrate the power of creativity and the amazing impact it has on our world. So, let's raise a glass (or a lyre) to these incredible ladies and the inspiration they bring!

Charites (Graces)

The Charites, or "Graces" as they're affectionately known, were three absolutely divine daughters of Zeus, born from his steamy affair with Eurynome, an Okeanid. These charming ladies, as gracious as they were gorgeous, brought an irresistible allure to various aspects of human life, from nature to art. When it came to parties, the Charites were the heart and soul, sprinkling delight and grace over every festivity. Honestly, no feast was complete without their enchanting presence to add that extra sparkle.

Now, let's dive deeper into the fabulous personalities of these divine sisters, who were famous for spreading joy and elegance wherever they went:

1. Aglaea: The youngest of the Charites, Aglaea was the personification of beauty, splendor, and glory. She had a gift for turning heads and leaving people dazzled by her radiant charm. Talk about making an entrance!

2. Euphrosyne: This vivacious middle sister was all about fun and laughter. Euphrosyne's contagious good spirits made her the life of the party, and everyone's go-to gal for a celebration or a night on the town.

3. Thalia: As the eldest of the Charites, Thalia embodied abundance and festivity. With her generous spirit and passion for lavish feasts, she made sure every gathering was not just memorable, but downright legendary.

The Charites loved to socialize with other gods and goddesses, often teaming up with the Muses to inspire creativity and joy in the arts. They were also BFFs with Aphrodite, the goddess of love and beauty, enhancing her already stunning aura with their own irresistible charm.

These graceful goddesses were frequently depicted in art, typically shown dancing and holding hands, symbolizing the harmony and unity they brought to every gathering. They also had a soft spot for nature, as their presence added beauty and delight to the world around them.

The Charites' characteristics make them truly delightful figures in Greek mythology. As the goddesses of charm, beauty, and grace, they remind us of the importance of spreading joy and kindness in our daily lives. Their influence touches everything from festivities and art to the natural world, inspiring us to embrace the beauty and pleasure life has to offer. So, let's raise a toast to the Charites, and let their enchanting spirit fill our hearts and homes with joy and grace!

Horai (Seasons)

Meet the Horai, a captivating trio of goddess sisters who played a pivotal role in ancient Greek mythology. As the embodiments of spring, summer, and winter, these charming daughters of Zeus and Themis held the keys to the natural order of the world. Thanks to their divine touch, life flourished, and agriculture boomed year-round. Let's delve into each Hora's unique characteristics and discover what made them so indispensable to the ancient Greeks.

1. Eunomia: Springing into action (pun intended), Eunomia was the personification of good order and harmony, both in nature and human society. As the goddess of spring, she ensured the earth was revitalized after a long winter, blessing the land with a kaleidoscope of blossoms and the irresistible scent of new life.

2. Dike: Turning up the heat as the Hora of summer, Dike symbolized justice, fair judgment, and moral order. She made sure the sun shone brightly, filling the days with warmth and providing the perfect conditions for crops to grow and thrive. Talk about a

ray of sunshine!

3. Eirene: Last but not least, Eirene represented winter, embodying peace, tranquility, and the serene beauty of a world blanketed in snow. As the goddess of winter, she offered a season of rest and reflection, allowing the earth to rejuvenate and prepare for the rebirth of spring.

But wait, there's more! The Horai weren't just seasonal sensations. They also served as the guardians of the gates of Mount Olympus, ensuring that the divine abode of the gods remained off-limits to unwanted guests. Plus, their connection to the orderly passage of the seasons made them the original timekeepers of the ancient Greek calendar.

In art and literature, the Horai were depicted as gorgeous, youthful women adorned with seasonal accessories like flowers, fruits, and cozy winter attire. Their grace and charm were believed to mirror the natural beauty they helped create in the world.

The Horai's unique characteristics make them truly enchanting figures in Greek mythology. As the goddesses of the seasons, they remind us of nature's ever-changing beauty and the importance of balance and harmony in both the natural world and human society. By honoring the Horai, we celebrate the endless cycle of life, growth, and renewal that sustains and nourishes us all. So, let's give a warm (or cool, depending on the season) welcome to these fabulous ladies and embrace the delightful gifts they bring to our world!

Nymphs

Ah, the Nymphs! These enchanting ladies simply cannot be overlooked in the world of Greek mythology. Frolicking in the mountains, waters, streams, springs, and meadows, Nymphs were the life and soul of the mythological party. Their name, meaning "young women of marriageable age," gives us a hint of their allure and charm. While they often played supportive or decorative roles in various myths, don't be deceived – these captivating creatures had plenty of their own stories to tell.

Let's dive into the characteristics of Nymphs and uncover the secrets behind their mystique:

- Nature Spirits: Nymphs were the ultimate nature spirits, each associated with a specific aspect of the natural world. From the Naiads, who called rivers and springs their home, to the Dryads, who dwelled within trees, Nymphs could be found in almost every corner of the earth, adding beauty and vitality to the world around them.

- Semi-Immortal: Though Nymphs lived much longer than mere mortals, they weren't considered truly immortal. Their lifespans were closely connected to the natural features they inhabited, so they could meet their end if their trees were cut down or their waters dried up. Talk about a vulnerability!

- Love Affairs: Nymphs, being as captivating as they were, often found themselves entangled in passionate love affairs – not just with humans, but also with gods and other mythical creatures. Some Nymphs even bore children to these lovers, adding a touch of divine drama to their stories.

- Shape-shifters: Some Nymphs were known to possess the ability to shape-shift, allowing them to transform into animals, plants, or other natural elements. This talent enabled them to blend seamlessly into their surroundings, making them the ultimate masters of disguise (and hide-and-seek!).

- Companions: Nymphs frequently served as attendants and companions to various gods and goddesses. For example, the Oceanids and Nereids accompanied Poseidon, the god of the sea, while the Oreads were often found in the company of Artemis, the goddess of the hunt. Quite the social butterflies, weren't they?

- Beauty and Grace: Nymphs were renowned for their stunning beauty and graceful demeanor. They were often depicted as young, beautiful women, radiating charm and allure that could make anyone swoon.

- Musical Talents: Many Nymphs were skilled in music and dance, often seen singing or playing instruments to entertain gods and goddesses during divine feasts or other celestial events. They definitely knew how to get the party started!

The Nymphs of Greek mythology were a captivating group of nature spirits, bringing beauty and charm to the world around them. Their semi-immortal status, love affairs, and other intriguing characteristics made them a fascinating addition to countless myths and legends. So, the next time you find yourself strolling through a lush forest or by a babbling brook, keep an eye out – you just might catch a glimpse of a playful Nymph enjoying the splendors of nature!

Satyrs

These peculiar and captivating creatures of Greek mythology were well-known for their wild, lustful nature and their mischievous antics. As half-human, half-animal beings, they were as fascinating as they were peculiar. With their unique appearance and cheeky behavior, they definitely stole the show. Let's explore the characteristics that made Satyrs the life of the mythological party:

- Hybrid Appearance: Sporting a distinctive hybrid look, Satyrs typically boasted the upper body of a man with the lower body of a horse, including horse hind legs and a swishing horse tail. Some Satyrs, however, also rocked goat-like features such as goat ears, horns, or legs. Their snobbish noses only added to their quirky charm.

- Mirthful and Lustful: With an insatiable appetite for revelry, feasting, and wine, Satyrs were notorious for their unbridled lust and merry, often tipsy behavior. They were frequently portrayed in a constant state of excitement, ready to turn any gathering into a wild celebration.

- Companions to Dionysus: Satyrs were often found keeping Dionysus, the god of wine and festivities, company. As embodiments of wildness and excess, they made perfect sidekicks for a god who loved to indulge in life's pleasures.

- Musicians and Dancers: Satyrs had a flair for music and dance, often depicted playing instruments like flutes, tambourines, or cymbals, and grooving to lively, frenzied dances.

- Notable Satyrs: Greek mythology featured several notable Satyrs, each with their own unique stories and characteristics. Marsyas, for example, was a musically talented Satyr who tragically met his demise after challenging the god Apollo to a musical contest. Pan, another half-human, half-goat character, was known for his lustful and irritable nature, especially if his afternoon snooze was interrupted. Other well-known Satyrs include Attis, Glaukos Pontios, Priapos, and Hymenaios.

- Tricksters: Satyrs were also infamous for their mischievous and sometimes sneaky nature. They loved to play tricks on both humans and gods, causing chaos and confusion wherever they roamed.

Satyrs were a truly unique and irresistible addition to Greek mythology. With their hybrid appearance, lustful demeanor, and love for mischief, they brought a sense of wildness and unpredictability to the myths they inhabited. So, the next time you stumble upon a story featuring these rambunctious beings, buckle up and get ready for a wild, entertaining ride!

CHAPTER 4

Demigods and Heroes

Demigods

Demigods, the fascinating offspring of divine and mortal parents, played an essential role in Greek mythology. Sporting divine attributes like their dashing good looks, unparalleled strength, and unique skills, demigods stood out in the crowd, like celebrities on the red carpet of ancient Greece.

In Greek mythology, demigods were truly one-of-a-kind. While other mythologies might feature the children of gods and mortals as mere mortals, the Greeks kicked it up a notch. Even though gods were practically a different species, they couldn't resist mingling with mortals. Zeus, Apollo, and the rest of the divine crew seemingly couldn't get enough of their mortal crushes. And boy, did they pay attention to their half-god, half-mortal offspring.

Demigods like Hercules and Perseus were the headliners of Greek myth. But they weren't the only ones—Jason's entourage on his journey to Colchis also boasted a fair share of demigods. So, what was the big deal with these divine-human hybrids?

Well, think of demigods as life coaches, courtesy of Greek mythology. The gods were supposed to be role models for humans, showing them how to live their best lives. But, let's be honest, they weren't exactly the epitome of moral excellence (looking at you, Zeus, with your wandering eyes and angry wife). The demigods, on the other hand, taught mortals how to embrace their inner divine nature, and perhaps even outshine the gods themselves.

Unlike tragic characters doomed to suffer from the get-go, demigods were larger-than-life heroes who overcame adversity to become more godlike than mere mortals. Sure, the gods had all the perks: superhuman strength, wisdom, immortality, and fabulous hair. But, demigods had to work for it, often starting life as "bastards" with absentee divine dads. Heroes like Perseus, Theseus, and even Achilles had to prove their worth by overcoming the gods' challenges.

Take Hercules, for example. This legendary demigod had the strength of a superhero, but life wasn't all sunshine and rainbows. He had to wrestle lions, outsmart lustful queens, and complete 12 seemingly impossible tasks, all while keeping up that classic Greek demigod smile. Talk about multitasking!

But, that's the point of demigod stories. These extraordinary characters demonstrated how humans could be more like gods—even better, perhaps. While gods rarely faced consequences for their bad behavior, humans did. The Greeks believed that this punishment was a key ingredient in the recipe for humanity. Life was tough, but with a little divine inspiration and a dash of demigod determination, mortals could achieve greatness and earn their heavenly rewards.

Greek Heroes

Perseus

Perseus, that dashing Greek hero we all know and love, was famous for his awe-inspiring acts of bravery and his noble sense of morality. At first, he thought being half-mortal made him weak, but he eventually realized that his human side actually gave him an edge. Born from the beautiful, albeit unconventional, union between the mortal princess Danae and the god Zeus, Perseus was blessed with divine powers to help him tackle countless challenges in his life.

Now, let's talk about his divine strength, one of his most impressive features. This muscle power came in handy when he faced formidable enemies like the petrifying Gorgon Medusa. Luckily for Perseus, the gods were rooting for him and gifted him with magical items to help him on his journey. He received Hermes' winged sandals, which gave him the ability to fly like a superhero; the Helm of Invisibility from Hades, which sounds like a must-have for any adventurer; and a shiny, reflective shield from Athena.

Perseus was also one courageous fellow. He'd never back down from a challenge, even if the odds seemed impossible. But it wasn't all about brute force with him. Nope, our hero had a quick wit and a resourceful mind that often saved the day. Take, for example, his mission to fetch Medusa's head. Instead of staring directly at the Gorgon and turning into a decorative statue, he cleverly used the reflective shield to view her reflection.

Throughout his adventures, Perseus showed an unwavering sense of justice and honor. He was always on a quest to protect the innocent and do the right thing. Like the time he saved Princess Andromeda from a ferocious sea monster. He stumbled upon her chained to a rock as a sacrifice, and without a moment's hesitation, he slayed the beast, rescued the damsel, and won her heart. Talk about a perfect love story! They eventually got hitched and returned to the Island of Serifos, where Perseus felt most at home.

Another thing that made Perseus so special was his compassion and empathy for others, traits that came from his human side. While he initially saw these qualities as weaknesses, they turned out to be real game-changers in his heroic journey. They helped him forge alliances and win the support of both gods and mortals alike.

So, there you have it! Perseus, an extraordinary hero, known for his divine strength, courage, resourcefulness, sense of justice, and empathy. Thanks to these attributes, he pulled off some truly epic feats and left a lasting impression on Greek mythology. And let's be honest, who wouldn't want a hero like that in their corner?

Hercules

Meet Hercules, the other big-shot hero in Greek mythology, widely regarded as the world's strongest man. He was born to the mighty Zeus and a mortal mother, the Theban princess Alcmene, so it's safe to say that greatness was in his genes. However, Hera, Zeus' not-so-thrilled wife, was pretty peeved about her husband's extracurricular activities and decided to take it out on baby Hercules. She sent two snakes to off the infant in his sleep, but to everyone's amazement, little Hercules grabbed those snakes by their throats and strangled them. Talk about an early display of talent! From that moment, it was clear that Hercules was destined to become a hero of both mortals and gods.

As Hercules grew up, he honed his combat skills, becoming an expert with the bow and arrow, the sword, and mastering the art of the hunt. However, he wasn't much of a fan of finer pursuits like poetry, literature, and music. In fact, he once accidentally killed his music teacher by whacking him with a lyre—clearly, he didn't know his own strength. To keep him out of trouble, Hercules was sent to the mountains, where he could flex his muscles without causing chaos.

In the mountains, our strapping young hero grew stronger and braver, and by the age of eighteen, he pulled off the incredible feat of killing a lion with his bare hands. But Hera's grudge was far from over. She was still fuming and, in her rage, caused Hercules to go mad, leading him to kill his own wife and children in a fit of insanity. To atone for his actions, Hercules sought guidance from the Oracle of Delphi and was instructed to follow the orders of Eurystheus, the King of Mycenae. This led to the legendary Labors of Hercules, a series of jaw-dropping feats that showcased his extraordinary strength and courage.

But Hercules wasn't just a muscle-bound hero. He had remarkable endurance, resilience, and determination that enabled him to tackle even the most intimidating tasks. As he completed his twelve labors, including capturing the elusive Ceryneian Hind, cleaning the notoriously filthy Augean stables, and even capturing Cerberus, the fearsome three-headed hound of the Underworld, Hercules proved himself to be quite the strategic thinker and problem-solver.

In addition to his brawn and brains, Hercules was known for his deep sense of loyalty, duty, and honor. No matter the obstacles he faced, he remained steadfast in his mission to redeem himself and serve the greater good. His compassion and empathy for others, qualities that often take a backseat in tales of heroism, played a vital role in helping him connect with mortals and gods alike.

So, there you have it! Hercules, an extraordinary figure in Greek mythology, celebrated for his phenomenal strength, courage, resilience, loyalty, and empathy. Through these attributes, he overcame countless challenges and left an indelible mark on the stories of ancient Greece. He's truly the kind of hero you'd want on your side in a pinch—or, you know, if you need help moving your couch.

Bellerophon

Bellerophon, the irresistibly charming nephew of the infamous Sisyphus, was born in Corinth, gifted with a divine trifecta of strength, grace, and drop-dead good looks. This Greek hero's tale began in his youth, when a tragic accident led to him accidentally killing a man. Desperate to wash his hands of the crime, Bellerophon set off for Tiryns, where the benevolent King Proetus kindly granted him absolution and welcomed him into the royal fold.

During his stay in Tiryns, Bellerophon's dashing charm caught the roving eye of Queen Anteia. Smitten with the handsome hero, she tried her best to woo him, but Bellerophon, ever the gentleman, tactfully declined her advances. In a classic case of love gone awry, the jilted queen spun a web of lies about Bellerophon, leaving her hubby less than pleased.

But Bellerophon's life was far from humdrum, and his jaw-dropping qualities went beyond his chiseled features. He was a formidable warrior, possessing an uncanny ability to tame even the wildest of beasts. His pièce de résistance? Taming the legendary winged horse, Pegasus, a feat no mortal had ever achieved. With Pegasus as his trusty sidekick, Bellerophon embarked on daring escapades, and his fame soared higher than his winged companion.

One of Bellerophon's most jaw-dropping accomplishments was his victory over the ferocious Chimera. This terrifying creature boasted the body of a lion, the tail of a serpent, and the head of a fire-breathing goat – the ultimate party-crasher! With a combination of brains and brawn, our hero managed to slay the monster and secure his spot in the hero hall of fame.

But every tale has its twists, and Bellerophon's pride eventually outgrew his better judgment. As his victories piled up, he started believing he was on the same level as the gods. In a moment of sheer overconfidence, he attempted to fly Pegasus to Mount Olympus, home of the gods. Zeus, however, was not amused by this mortal's audacity. He sent an irksome gadfly to sting Pegasus, causing the horse to buck and send Bellerophon hurtling to the ground.

Though Bellerophon survived the fall, his life took a tragic turn. Crippled and disgraced, he wandered the earth, lonely and abandoned by the gods. And so, Bellerophon's tale stands as an ageless reminder to keep our pride in check, or face the dire consequences of thinking we can hobnob with the divine.

Theseus

Theseus, a Greek hero with a flair for the dramatic and a family tree that boasts both mortal and divine branches, is best known for taking down the fearsome Minotaur and uniting Attica under Athens. This legendary lad had not one but two dads: Aegeus, the king of Athens, and Poseidon, the god of seas (talk about some serious paternal pressure!).

Desperate for an heir but clueless about how to make it happen, Aegeus consulted the Oracle of Delphi for some parental advice. The Oracle's cryptic response left him scratching his head, so he turned to King Pittheus of Troezen for wisdom. In a classic case of miscommunication, instead of providing a clear answer, Pittheus introduced Aegeus to his lovely daughter, Aethra. Fast-forward to their wedding night, when Aethra found herself seduced by Poseidon on the island of Sphairia. The result? A child with a potent blend of mortal charm and divine mojo.

When Aethra became pregnant, Aegeus decided to head back to Athens. But before leaving, he buried his sandals and sword under a rock as a test for his future offspring, telling Aethra that once their son was strong enough to move the stone and retrieve the items, he'd be ready to claim his birthright. Aegeus then abandoned Aethra and returned to Athens to marry Medea, a sorceress with a penchant for vengeance. This revolving door of relationships may have rubbed off on Theseus, who developed a knack for leaving a string of heartbroken women in his wake.

Growing up under his mother's watchful eye, Theseus remained in the dark about his father's identity until he hit sixteen and muscled his way past the rock to uncover the hidden sandals and sword. Aethra then spilled the beans, urging him to take the items to Aegeus and claim his place in the family.

Theseus had two options for his journey to Athens: a quick and safe sea voyage, or a dangerous land route that would involve skirting the Saronic Gulf and facing six fearsome guardians of the underworld. Never one to shy away from a challenge, Theseus chose the latter.

As he embarked on his perilous quest, Theseus showcased remarkable courage, strength, and cunning, dispatching each guardian with flair. But his pièce de résistance was his nail-biting showdown with the Minotaur, a half-man, half-bull monstrosity that lurked in the twisted labyrinth of King Minos. With brains and brawn, Theseus managed to slay the beast and escape the maze, earning himself a spot in the hero hall of fame.

But Theseus wasn't just about flexing his muscles; he was also a forward-thinking leader who unified Attica under Athens' rule. His efforts to bring the region together laid the foundation for Athens' rise as a major power in ancient Greece. Theseus' legacy as a hero, adventurer, and progressive leader continues to enchant and inspire generations, proving that a little divine intervention, determination, and a healthy dose of humor can go a long way.

Jason

Jason, our Greek hero, was known for his epic quest as the commander of a magical ship, the Argo, in search of the fabled Golden Fleece. Born to Aeson, a king in Thessaly, Northern Greece, Jason's life took a soap-opera-worthy turn when his father was overthrown by none other than his own brother, the not-so-cuddly Uncle Pelias. This power-hungry uncle threatened to take out anyone who dared to challenge his claim to the throne.

To keep Jason safe from Pelias' clutches, he was whisked away and placed under the watchful eye of Chiron, a friendly centaur with a gift for mentoring heroes. As Jason grew into a dashing young man, he decided it was time to grab the bull by the horns and reclaim his kingdom. During his journey, he showcased his gentlemanly side by helping an elderly woman cross a river. Little did he know, this kind-hearted act would gain him a powerful ally, as the woman was actually the goddess Hera in disguise. Touched by his gallantry, she vowed to support Jason in his future endeavors.

While assisting the incognito Hera, Jason had a minor fashion mishap, losing one of his sandals. This fact would soon propel him into the adventure of a lifetime. You see, Pelias had been warned by a prophecy to watch out for a one-sandaled stranger. When Jason rocked up with a single sandal, Pelias knew the prophecy had come to pass. Desperate to keep his throne, he sent Jason on a near-impossible quest to fetch the Golden Fleece, thinking it would be curtains for our hero.

But Jason was far from alone in his daring quest. With some divine help from the goddesses Hera and Athena, he commissioned the construction of the legendary ship Argo and assembled a dream team of fifty valiant warriors. This star-studded crew included the mighty Hercules, the twin brothers Castor and Pollux, the melodious Orpheus, and the swift-footed Atalanta. Together, they set sail for the distant land of Colchis on the Black Sea.

Facing daunting odds, Jason and his band of Argonauts embarked on a rollercoaster adventure brimming with danger, suspense, and more than a few unexpected twists. Their journey tested their courage, wits, and determination as they tackled obstacles like clashing rocks and fire-breathing bulls. Through it all, Jason's leadership and resilience shone like a beacon, proving that even a hero with just one sandal could leave an indelible mark on the pages of Greek mythology.

Achilles

Achilles, the legendary Greek warrior and star of Homer's epic poem, the Iliad, was quite the hero back in the day. Born to the mortal king Peleus and the sea nymph Thetis, Achilles was destined for greatness from the get-go. With divine ancestry and a prophecy in his favor, he was basically the ancient Greek version of a celebrity, set to become the most fearsome warrior of his time.

To give her son an edge in battle, Thetis decided to dip Achilles into the River Styx, gripping him by his heel—talk about a daring parenting move! As a result, his heel became his only vulnerable spot. This "Achilles' heel," as it would later be known, would play a rather significant role in his life.

Achilles' education was top-notch, with the wise centaur Chiron as his tutor, teaching him the art of combat and the values of a true warrior. As he grew older, Achilles' reputation as a fearsome fighter spread across Greece like wildfire, and he was soon recruited to join the Greek forces in the Trojan War. It was during this war that Achilles would achieve his greatest glory and face his ultimate tragedy.

Leading the Myrmidons, an elite group of warriors from his homeland of Phthia, Achilles quickly became the MVP of the Greek army. His unparalleled skills in battle, combined with his ferocity and determination, made him a force to be reckoned with. However, Achilles had a bit of a temper, which often led to conflicts with his fellow Greeks, most notably with King Agamemnon.

As the Trojan War raged on, Achilles' anger and pride eventually led him to throw a legendary tantrum, withdrawing from the battlefield and leaving his comrades to face the Trojans without him. It took the death of his best friend, Patroclus, to snap Achilles out of his funk and send him back into the fight, thirsting for vengeance.

In a series of epic battles, Achilles sent the Trojan hero Hector to the afterlife and avenged Patroclus' death. But, as with all good stories, Achilles' victory was short-lived. The Trojan prince, Paris, managed to land a lucky shot on our hero's vulnerable heel with a well-aimed arrow.

Achilles' story serves as a powerful reminder of the duality of human nature, showcasing both the glory and tragedy that can result from our passions and desires. Despite his untimely end, Achilles remains an iconic figure in Greek mythology, representing the very essence of heroism and the never-ending struggle between our strengths and weaknesses.

Ulysses

Ulysses, also known as Odysseus, was a legendary Greek hero who had a real knack for getting into (and out of) sticky situations. As the protagonist of Homer's epic poem, the Odyssey, Ulysses became the poster boy for adventure and perseverance, securing his spot as one of the most iconic figures in Greek lore.

Born to King Laertes and Queen Anticlea of Ithaca, Ulysses was destined for greatness from the get-go. His education and training were top-notch, ensuring that he grew up to be a skilled warrior, a smooth talker, and a cunning strategist. These traits would serve him well when he received his invitation to the ultimate Greek showdown: the Trojan War.

While Ulysses' battlefield prowess was certainly nothing to sneeze at, it was his cunning mind that truly set him apart from his peers. After all, he was the genius behind the famous Trojan Horse, a brilliant scheme that led to Troy's epic faceplant. With the war won, Ulysses set sail for home, eager to reunite with his wife, Penelope, and their son, Telemachus.

Unfortunately for our hero, the journey back to Ithaca would prove to be more challenging than finding a parking spot in downtown Athens. Over the course of a decade, Ulysses and his crew faced a series of seemingly insurmountable obstacles, including vengeful gods, monstrous creatures, and enchantresses who probably should've had their magic licenses revoked. Through it all, Ulysses' wit, courage, and sheer determination enabled him to overcome each challenge, albeit at a considerable cost.

By the time Ulysses finally reached the shores of Ithaca, he had lost his entire crew and was practically unrecognizable. However, his trials were far from over. Upon his return, he found his home infested with suitors vying for Penelope's hand in marriage, believing Ulysses to be as dead.

Undeterred, Ulysses disguised himself as a beggar, infiltrated his own palace, and ultimately sent the unwelcome guests packing with a mix of cunning and good old-fashioned butt-kicking.

With his home reclaimed and his family reunited, Ulysses' legendary odyssey came to a triumphant close. His incredible journey serves as a testament to the power of human ingenuity, perseverance, and the indomitable spirit of adventure. So the next time you find yourself facing a seemingly insurmountable challenge, just remember the tale of Ulysses and remind yourself that sometimes, even the longest, craziest odysseys can have happy endings.

Oedipus

Oedipus, the legendary Greek hero who just couldn't catch a break, serves as the tragic centerpiece of Sophocles' renowned play, "Oedipus Rex." The poor guy's story is a cautionary tale that reminds us of the pitfalls of hubris, the limits of human understanding, and the inescapable nature of destiny. Talk about a tough life!

Born to King Laius and Queen Jocasta of Thebes, Oedipus was doomed from the get-go. When a prophecy claimed he'd grow up to kill dear old dad and marry his mom, his parents took some extreme measures to prevent this disastrous outcome. They had baby Oedipus' feet pierced and bound and then ordered a shepherd to abandon him on a mountainside to die. Harsh, right?

But as fate would have it, the shepherd had a soft spot and spared the infant, handing him over to a childless royal couple from the nearby kingdom of Corinth. They raised Oedipus as their own, never spilling the beans about his true origins.

As he grew up, Oedipus also heard the spine-chilling prophecy and, believing his adoptive parents were his birth parents, hightailed it out of Corinth to dodge his destiny. Oh, the irony! That very decision led him straight into the arms of tragedy.

On his travels, Oedipus got into a heated argument with a man at a crossroads and killed him. Little did he know, the man was his biological father, King Laius. Continuing on his journey, Oedipus arrived in Thebes, which was plagued by the Sphinx, a monstrous creature with the body of a lion, the wings of an eagle, and the head of a woman. The Sphinx posed riddles to travelers, and if they failed to answer correctly, it was mealtime.

Using his smarts and resourcefulness, Oedipus cracked the Sphinx's riddle, saving Thebes and earning the citizens' gratitude. They offered him the now-empty throne and the hand of their widowed queen, Jocasta. Unaware of their true relationship, Oedipus married his own mother, fulfilling that cringe-worthy prophecy.

Years later, a plague struck Thebes, and Oedipus, as the respected king, vowed to find the cause and save his city. After a series of investigations and jaw-dropping revelations, Oedipus finally uncovered the truth about his identity and the horrific deeds he had unknowingly committed. Overcome with grief and horror, Jocasta took her own life, and Oedipus, in a fit of despair, blinded himself.

Oedipus' story is a poignant reminder of the intricate dance between fate, free will, and human understanding. It stands as a testament to the power of unintended consequences and the tragic irony that sometimes the very actions we take to avoid disaster can lead us directly into its clutches.

Monsters, Hybrids & Giants

In the wild and wacky world of Greek mythology, it's not all about gods, goddesses, and spirits. Nope, there's a whole other cast of characters that'll make your jaw drop and your imagination run wild. We're talking about the monsters, hybrids, and giants, folks! These semi-divine creatures are often closely related to the gods themselves and play a big part in the myths and legends we still love today. So, buckle up and get ready for a fantastical ride through the strange and captivating realm of Greek mythological creatures.

Mentioned below are some of the creatures that hold importance in Greek Mythology.

Typhoeous

Typhoeous, also known as Typhon, was the kind of monstrous giant that could make even the most daring heroes second-guess their career choices. With a wingspan that put jumbo jets to shame, Typhoeous was so colossal that his head practically grazed the stars. But don't be fooled by his astronomical connections – this creature was a force you didn't want to mess with.

This spine-chilling behemoth had an origin story with more drama than a reality TV show. You see, his mother, Gaea, was feeling rather peeved after her children, the Titans, were booted from the heavens by Zeus. Like any overprotective parent, she decided that the perfect way to get back at the king of the gods was to give birth to the ultimate weapon of mass destruction: Typhoeous.

As Typhoeous made his grand entrance, his very presence sent shivers down the spines of gods and mortals alike. With his immense size, terrifying appearance, and unparalleled power, Typhoeous seemed like just the right guy to give Zeus a taste of his own medicine. And for a while, it looked like Gaea's plan might actually succeed.

But Zeus, never one to shy away from a challenge, wasn't about to let this monster steal his thunder. In an epic battle, Zeus and Typhoeous went head-to-head, with the fate of the universe hanging in the balance. In the end, Zeus emerged victorious, thanks in no small part to his trusty lightning bolts, which he used to vanquish the fearsome giant.

Hecatoncheires

In Greek mythology, the Hecatoncheires were like the original multitaskers – and no, we're not talking about their ability to juggle careers in singing, dancing, and acting. These monstrous triplets, born to Gaea and Uranus, really knew how to turn heads – 50 of them, to be exact, per sibling – and with 100 hands each.

Despite their many hands, life wasn't all back rubs and applause for the Hecatoncheires, particularly during the reign of the Titans. In a twist of fate that would make any soap opera jealous, they found themselves banished to Tartarus, a place that made Alcatraz look like a day spa. There, they languished in darkness, dreaming of the day they'd break free.

Enter Zeus, the god with a knack for grand gestures and a heart for underdogs. Recognizing the untapped potential of the Hecatoncheires, Zeus busted them out of their Tartarus prison. Eager to express their gratitude and return the favor, the Hecatoncheires vowed to give Zeus a hand (or two, or a hundred) in his divine power struggle.

The stage was set for the epic clash known as Titanomachy, and the Hecatoncheires were ready to play their part. Catching the Titans off guard with a surprise attack, they made the most of their numerous hands, overwhelming their opponents and ultimately helping Zeus and the other Olympians clinch victory.

Cyclopes

In the fantastical realm of Greek mythology, the Cyclopes were a trio that would definitely catch your eye – and not just because they were unusually tall or fashionable. No, these three immortal giants were hard to miss due to the single, massive eye centered in the middle of their foreheads. As the offspring of Gaea and Uranus, these uniquely visaged giants stood out from the crowd.

Life, however, wasn't always a bed of roses for the Cyclopes. Their early days were anything but a walk in the park, thanks to their father Uranus. You see, he wasn't exactly a fan of their one-of-a-kind appearance, so he took a rather unconventional parenting approach: he shoved them right back into Gaea as soon as they were born.

Luckily for the Cyclopes, the Titans eventually stepped in to save the day. They yanked them out of Gaea and whisked them away to the not-so-glamorous destination known as Tartarus. There, the Cyclopes bided their time, waiting for a chance to turn their fortunes around.

That big break finally arrived in the form of Titanomachy, the colossal showdown between the Titans and the Olympians. Zeus, always on the lookout for powerful allies, decided to spring the Cyclopes from their Tartarus incarceration. In a show of gratitude, the Cyclopes crafted some seriously awe-inspiring lightning bolts for their savior, Zeus.

With these electrifying weapons at his disposal, Zeus triumphed over the Titans, securing his place as king of the gods. The Cyclopes' story serves as a reminder that sometimes, having friends with unconventional talents – and even more unconventional looks – can be a real game-changer. So next time you come across someone who stands out from the crowd, think of the Cyclopes, the one-eyed giants who turned the tide of battle with a little help from their lightning bolts.

Sphinx

The Sphinx, that mysterious creature from Greek mythology, was quite the conversation starter with its unique ensemble of animal parts. Imagine a human head perched on a lion's body, sporting the wings of an eagle and a tail adorned with a serpent. Quite the head-turner, wouldn't you agree?

But the Sphinx wasn't all about looks – this creature also had a flair for riddles that would leave even the brainiest of scholars utterly befuddled. And if someone failed to crack her riddles? Well, let's just say she had a taste for those who couldn't keep up, literally devouring them on the spot.

In one particularly gripping tale, our hero Oedipus managed to achieve the unthinkable – he solved the Sphinx's riddle! Flabbergasted by this turn of events, the Sphinx had a bit of a meltdown and hurled herself into the ocean. Sure, it might seem like a dramatic response, but who can blame her? Nobody enjoys losing, after all.

Now, if the Greek Sphinx rings a bell, it's probably because she has a twin of sorts in Egyptian mythology. The most renowned Sphinx of all is the awe-inspiring limestone statue in Giza, a gigantic 240 feet long and 66 feet high wonder. Crafted between 2558 and 2532 BCE, this age-old enigma still captivates tourists and scholars alike, all eager to unravel the secrets of this captivating creature.

Hydra

Imagine a creature so terrifying that even the boldest of heroes would think twice before picking a fight. Allow us to introduce the Hydra, a monstrous water snake with not just one, but a whole bunch of heads. And as if that wasn't hair-raising enough, the Hydra had an uncanny party trick up its sleeve – lop off one of its heads, and voilà! Two more would sprout back in its place. Now that's what I call a never-ending nightmare!

You might be tempted to think that the Hydra was unbeatable, and for most mortals, that would be true. But there was one hero who dared to take up the challenge: Hercules. This legendary demigod faced the Lernaean Hydra in one of his renowned Twelve Labors, a series of epic tasks designed to test his strength and courage.

But Hercules wasn't just some muscle-bound hero; he had a few clever tricks up his sleeve when it came to battling the formidable Hydra. By harnessing a winning combination of brawn and brains, he ultimately managed to outwit the slippery serpent and triumph against all odds.

Chimera

Hold onto your hats, because just when you thought mythical creatures couldn't get any weirder, along comes the Chimera to redefine bizarre. Imagine a monster with the body and head of a lion, a tail that morphs into a snake, and – just for good measure – a goat's head sprouting from its back – a truly eclectic mix that makes Frankenstein's monster look like a run-of-the-mill science experiment. Oh, and did we mention this fearsome beast can also breathe fire? Yeah, you might want to keep a safe distance from this one.

The ancient Greeks were truly the Picassos of the mythical creature world, and the Chimera is a prime example of their wild imaginations at work. This legendary monster didn't just stay within the confines of Greece, though; its hair-raising reputation traveled far and wide, inspiring other cultures to welcome the Chimera into their own pantheon of creepy creatures.

In today's world, the term "chimera" has evolved beyond its monstrous roots, now used to describe anything that's so fantastical, spine-chilling, or downright bizarre that it seems too unreal to exist. The Chimera – living proof that sometimes, the most extraordinary things are born from the wildest of imaginations.

Pegasus

Imagine a truly majestic creature that stands out among the mythical beings of ancient Greece. It's a snow-white horse, so pure and pristine that it could only be described as regal. But wait, there's more – this horse has wings! That's right, we're talking about Pegasus, the incredible flying horse that captured the imaginations of the Greeks, soaring through their myths with grace and elegance.

The origin of Pegasus is just as fascinating as its appearance. When the hero Perseus scored a major win against the dreaded Medusa by lopping off her snake-covered head, a single drop of her blood did something quite unexpected – it transformed into the first Pegasus. Clearly not your average horse, Pegasus decided that a simple life on Earth just wasn't going to cut it. So, with a flap of his wings, he soared straight to Mount Olympus, offering his services to the big boss himself, Zeus. Needless to say, the king of the gods was more than happy to welcome such a magnificent creature into the divine crew.

While Pegasus may not be a god or demi-god, he's no run-of-the-mill monster, either. In fact, one Greek story tells of Pegasus bravely going head-to-head with the Chimera, proving that this winged wonder has a heroic streak. Soaring through the skies and capturing the hearts of mortals and gods alike, Pegasus shows that when it comes to mythical creatures, sometimes all you need is a little bit of goodness, a dash of courage, and a whole lot of style.

Sirens

The Sirens may seem like a charming bunch of gals at first glance, but don't let their enchanting appearance fool you – they're master manipulators. These mesmerizing seabird women set up shop on islands and rocky outcrops, using their irresistible songs to lure unsuspecting sailors to their doom. Their melodies are so captivating that even the most seasoned seafarers can't help but jump ship, trying to reach the source of the bewitching tunes. Sadly, these poor souls are never seen again. Some Greeks believed the Sirens gobbled them up, while others thought they simply drowned. Either way, listening to a Siren's song was a one-way ticket to the underworld.

The Sirens make a splash in two famous Greek tales: The Odyssey and Jason and the Argonauts. In The Odyssey, the resourceful Ulysses and his crew sail past the Sirens' island. To avoid succumbing to their alluring voices, Ulysses orders his men to plug their ears with beeswax. But the ever-curious Ulysses can't resist a sneak peek – or rather, a sneak listen. He asks to be tied to the ship's mast so he can hear the song without jumping overboard. When the Sirens' tune drives him wild with desire, his crew wisely ignores his pleas for release, and they sail past the island unscathed.

In Jason and the Argonauts, the Sirens make an encore appearance. This time, instead of beeswax, Jason arms himself with a secret weapon: a musician who plays at full volume to drown out the Sirens' deadly serenade. His plan almost works, but one crew member's ears prove too sharp for his own good. He leaps overboard, lured by the briefest snippet of the Sirens' song. Luckily, Aphrodite swoops in and saves him from a soggy demise.

The Sirens, with their seductive voices and treacherous charm, serve as a cautionary tale in Greek mythology. They remind us that sometimes even the most enchanting beauty can conceal a dangerous trap.

Harpies

Harpies, those mythical creatures with a truly distinctive and captivating appearance, have been fascinating folks for ages. These creatures are often depicted as having the body of a bird, with a woman's head and face. They have sharp, curved talons on their feet, which make them formidable predators in the world of mythology. Harpies also possess strong, feathered wings, allowing them to soar through the skies with great speed and agility.

Don't be fooled by their enchanting faces, though. While they may draw you in with their mesmerizing beauty, harpies have a terrifying screeching voice that could send shivers down anyone's spine.

But wait, there's more! Harpies have a special trick up their wing – they can summon mighty winds to help them swoop down and snatch unsuspecting victims.

Often seen as agents of punishment and vengeance, these winged wonders have a bit of a bad rep. Some legends even paint them as divine retribution enforcers. With their fierce wings, it's no wonder they've come to symbolize the destructive forces of nature, like storms and whirlwinds.

Despite their fearsome and terrifying nature, harpies have managed to capture our imagination throughout history. They've become popular subjects in art, literature, and mythology.

Erinyes

The Erinyes, or as they're more commonly known, the Furies – mythical creatures with a penchant for vengeance that have captured human imagination for eons. When it comes to doling out justice to those who've committed dastardly deeds against family members, these supernatural sisters don't play around. They're the embodiment of divine justice, and they have a unique skill set that lets them do their job with unfaltering efficiency.

Hailing from Greek mythology, the Erinyes consist of three fearsome sisters: Alecto, Megaera, and Tisiphone. They're renowned for their dark, ominous appearance – think shadowy wings sprouting from their backs and serpents entwined in their hair. This spine-chilling look is basically a "Do Not Disturb" sign for anyone thinking about breaking the rules and committing heinous acts.

These ladies are no ordinary avengers. The Erinyes possess incredible strength, agility, and the power of flight, which they use to chase down their targets with dogged determination. They also have a nose for guilt, literally sniffing out wrongdoers and tracing the stench back to its source. And when they find their prey, they use a mix of psychological and physical torment to drive the guilty party to the edge of insanity – ensuring they get what's coming to them.

But the Erinyes aren't just about looks and chasing down ne'er-do-wells. They also have a deep connection to the afterlife. It's said they reside in the depths of the Underworld, hanging out with Hades and his better half, Persephone. Their job down there? Making sure that wicked souls receive their eternal comeuppance, a not-so-gentle reminder that justice doesn't stop at the mortal realm.

The Erinyes have made their mark on human culture and mythology, and their hair-raising tales continue to inspire those drawn to the darker side of the supernatural. While their methods might be a tad extreme, the Erinyes serve as a stark reminder that justice matters, and messing with the moral order can have dire consequences.

Centaurs

Centaurs, those legendary half-human, half-horse hybrids, have been cantering through mythology and human imagination for eons. Famous for their dual nature, they showcase a captivating mix of human smarts and animal instincts, making them real standouts among mythical creatures.

Straight from the pages of Greek mythology, centaurs are usually portrayed with the torso of a human and the body of a horse. Talk about the best of both worlds! This one-of-a-kind combo gives them the perks of human intelligence along with the strength and speed of a powerful stallion.

Centaurs are quite the enigmatic bunch. Some are known for their wisdom and scholarly pursuits, while others are, well, party animals. This fascinating duality is exemplified by the famous centaur Chiron, who was a top-notch teacher and mentor to Greek heroes like Achilles and

Hercules.

When it comes to finding a home, centaurs prefer the great outdoors. Their stomping grounds can usually be found in the lush forests and mountains of Thessaly in Greece. These nature-loving hybrids are skilled hunters, archers, and horse whisperers (no surprise there). Their extraordinary talents have inspired countless legendary tales that continue to enthral audiences today.

Centaurs haven't just made a splash in ancient mythology, but they've also left their hoofprints on various art forms, literature, and pop culture. From renaissance masterpieces to modern fantasy novels and movies, centaurs keep on galloping through our collective consciousness, reminding us of the delicate balance between our human intellect and our more primal urges.

Cerberus

Cerberus, the fearsome yet fabulous guardian of the Underworld, has been growling his way through mythology and human imagination for ages. With his imposing presence and unwavering loyalty to the god Hades, Cerberus is the ultimate symbol of protection and serves as a formidable bouncer for any would-be party crashers.

Straight out of Greek mythology, Cerberus is typically depicted as a massive, monstrous dog with multiple heads – usually three, but sometimes more, just for a little extra "oomph" of terror. With a serpent's tail and snakes slithering from his mane, this hellhound is truly a sight that's hard to forget. This one-of-a-kind appearance not only makes Cerberus the ultimate conversation starter but also allows him to keep a watchful eye (or six) on the entrance to the Underworld.

Cerberus has a reputation for being fierce and fiercely loyal. As the dedicated gatekeeper of the Underworld, he ensures that the souls of the deceased stay put and prevents the living from sneaking in uninvited. This devoted guardian takes his job very seriously – after all, you wouldn't want to get on the bad side of the god of the dead.

The stomping grounds of Cerberus, the Underworld, is a dark and mysterious place where the souls of the departed reside. Ruled by Hades and his queen, Persephone, the Underworld is a rather inhospitable realm where Cerberus' ferocious presence serves as both a warning to unwanted guests and a source of comfort for those seeking a little order amidst chaos.

Cerberus has left his paw prints on various aspects of human culture and mythology, captivating the hearts of supernatural enthusiasts everywhere. From ancient art and literature to modern films and video games, this legendary hellhound continues to snarl his way through our collective consciousness, reminding us of the importance of loyalty and the consequences of crossing boundaries.

Minotaur

The Minotaur, a legendary creature with an extraordinary and somewhat intimidating presence, has captured the imagination of countless people over the centuries. This formidable hybrid beast, boasting the body of a man and the head of a bull, perfectly embodies the essence of raw strength and primal instincts.

Born from the rather unusual union of Queen Pasiphae and a spectacular bull, the Minotaur's tragic origin story is as fascinating as it is bizarre. Blessed (or cursed) with an insatiable appetite for human flesh, this fearsome creature was ultimately locked away within a mind-bending labyrinth by King Minos of Crete. Designed by the ingenious architect Daedalus, this intricate maze served not only to hide the Minotaur from the world but also to prevent his monstrous nature from wreaking havoc on unsuspecting citizens.

The Minotaur is renowned for its awe-inspiring strength and ferocity, striking fear (and possibly an odd fascination) into the hearts of those who cross its path. A unique blend of human cunning and the raw power of a bull, the Minotaur is nothing short of a mythological powerhouse. Let's just say you wouldn't want to invite this beast to a dinner party, unless you wanted to be the main course!

The labyrinth that houses the Minotaur stands as a symbol of the complexity and mystery that surrounds this enigmatic creature. Its maze-like corridors and seemingly endless passages serve as a metaphor for the challenges we face in understanding our own primal instincts and the darker aspects of human nature. After all, who among us hasn't found themselves lost in the twisty-turny mess of our own thoughts?

The Minotaur has left an indelible mark on various aspects of human culture and mythology, serving as a source of inspiration and intrigue for generations. With its unforgettable appearance and raw power, this legendary beast reminds us that there's often more to us than meets the eye—and that sometimes, the most captivating mysteries can be found within the depths of our own labyrinthine souls.

Medusa

Medusa, that infamous figure from Greek mythology, holds a special place in the nightmares of many. This Gorgon's gaze packs a punch – one look, and you'll find yourself a permanent statue. But what makes her so memorable? Let's dive into the details of her distinctive features, which have captured the imagination of countless generations.

First up, Medusa's crowning glory (or horror, depending on how you see it) is her head of slithering, venomous snakes. These wriggling, hissing reptiles create an atmosphere that's equal parts unsettling and oddly mesmerizing.

Now, about those eyes. They say the eyes are the windows to the soul, but with Medusa, one look and you're stone-cold. Her powerful, petrifying gaze makes her a formidable figure. Not even the most skilled warriors can resist being turned into lawn ornaments if they happen to catch her stare.

Another feature of Medusa's appearance is her sharp, fang-like teeth. These teeth not only add to her monstrous visage but also serve as a reminder of her predatory nature. After all, this is one lady you don't want to mess with.

Her complexion also deserves a mention. Medusa sports a pale, sickly hue that gives her an otherworldly, ghostly vibe. This pallor sets her apart from mere mortals, reinforcing her status as a supernatural and monstrous being.

But don't be fooled by her terrifying features. Medusa is also said to possess an alluring beauty, which only adds to her mystique. The contrast between her hair-raising (or snake-raising) aspects and her captivating charm make her an enigmatic and fascinating figure in Greek mythology. You could say she's the ultimate femme fatale – just be sure not to look her in the eyes!

CHAPTER 5

The Most Compelling And Fascinating Myths

Ade and Persephone: The Myth of the Seasons

On the dizzying Mount Olympus, there was a young and radiant deity. She was the goddess of spring, whose beauty enchanted the male deities. Her name was Kora, but she would become more known as Persephone.

Persephone's mother, Demeter, the goddess of agriculture, was overly protective and kept her daughter away from the intrigues of the Olympians. She wanted to preserve her purity and virginity, just as the goddesses Athena, Artemis, and Hestia had done. Therefore, Demeter did everything she could to keep Aphrodite and her son Eros, the deities of love, away from her daughter.

However, these two were not willing to accept the existence of another deity in Olympus immune to their influence. Thus, they devised a plan to inflame the heart of young Persephone.

Meanwhile, far from Olympus, in the depths of the earth, lived another god free from the influence of the deities of love. It was Hades, lord of the Underworld, who busily dealt with his numerous tasks without having time to be distracted by anything else.

One day, a sudden earthquake shook the realm of Hades, who ascended to the surface to see what was happening. Mount Etna was erupting, a sign that Typhon, the monster imprisoned by Zeus, was particularly unhappy. It was then that he heard a sweet voice coming from a nearby forest. There, in the woods, Persephone was singing, unaware of being observed.

Noticing Hades' interest in Persephone, Aphrodite and Eros decided to seize the opportunity. With one of his golden arrows, which infused desire and passion into the hearts of men and gods, Eros struck Hades' heart.

Consumed by passion, Hades approached the goddess of spring, who, surprised, tried to resist. But Hades, impetuous, grabbed the young woman and the earth opened a passage to his kingdom.

With the goddess in his arms, Hades was descending into his kingdom when Demeter realized her daughter's absence. She began to search for Persephone everywhere, and after much searching, she found one of the nymphs who had witnessed the abduction.

Discovering that Hades had kidnapped Persephone and taken her to the Underworld, Demeter was seized with anger. To punish Gaia, the earth goddess who had allowed Hades to kidnap her daughter, she decided to render the earth barren. Thus, the earth became arid and the crops ceased.

Zeus, worried about the situation because if Demeter no longer performed her duties, chaos would take over the world, tried to convince Demeter to return to her duties, but she insisted that the world would remain barren until she had her daughter back. Zeus assured her that Persephone would be released unless she had eaten any fruit from the underworld. So, Zeus instructed Hermes to bring Demeter to Hades' realm to recover Persephone.

But once there, Demeter found Persephone eating pomegranate seeds offered by Hades. After eating them, Persephone became the queen of the Underworld, bound to that realm forever.

Demeter scolded her daughter for agreeing to eat the food offered by Hades, but Persephone replied that Hades wasn't so bad, he treated her with respect and genuinely loved her.

Seeing Demeter's despair, Hades proposed a deal: Persephone would spend half of the year in the Underworld and the other half on the surface with her mother.

Accepting the deal, Persephone returned to the surface with her mother and the earth bloomed again, and crops were once again abundant. However, when it was time for Persephone to return to the Underworld,

Demeter, in despair, again left the earth to fend for itself, neglecting her duties. And so, with the departures and returns of Persephone, the seasons were born.

Orpheus and Eurydice

The ancient Greek world was teeming with musicians and poets, who sang the exploits of gods and heroes, yet among them shone an unparalleled talent: Orpheus. Offspring of the Muse Calliope and the God Apollo, Orpheus had inherited from his mother a melodious and unmatched voice, and from his father an extraordinary gift for musical composition.

It was as if the universe itself had fallen silent to listen to Orpheus play his lyre, a gift from his father Apollo. When the notes wafted into the air, animals calmed down, lulled by the sound, and even the plants seemed to sway to the rhythm of the music, in a silent ballet. But Orpheus was not just a virtuoso artist: within him burned the courage worthy of a hero.

And it was this courage that led Orpheus to join Jason's crew in his daring quest for the Golden Fleece. During this adventure, the Argonauts found themselves facing the dangerous melody of the sirens. But thanks to Orpheus's music, sweeter and more captivating than any seductive song, the crew managed to escape their deadly charm.

Upon his return from the odyssey, Orpheus locked eyes with the beautiful Eurydice, and his heart took flight. Eurydice, in turn, became the greatest admirer of Orpheus's songs, so much so that the hero sometimes felt even jealous of his own compositions, which so intensely captivated his beloved's attention.

During their wedding, dark omens cast a shadow over their happiness. Despite this, the couple decided to face the future with courage, determined to live each day to the fullest. But tragedy was lurking: as Eurydice was walking in the fields, Aristaeus, a beekeeper, attempted to abuse her. In her flight, Eurydice was bitten by a venomous snake hidden in the tall grass. Orpheus reached her in time to hold her one last time in his arms, before she sank into the underworld.

From that moment, Orpheus's lyre no longer emitted sweet melodies, but only cries of despair. The pain of losing Eurydice was so great that Orpheus decided to defy the laws of Olympus, begging Zeus to bring his beloved back to life. Zeus, however, refused, but suggested to Orpheus to go himself to the world of the dead and speak directly to Hades, the lord of the underworld.

So, Orpheus descended into the world of the dead, accompanied by Hermes, the messenger of the gods. With his music he softened the heart of Charon, the boatman, convincing him to carry him across the river of the dead. He managed to appease Cerberus, the fierce three-headed dog guarding the entrance of the underworld, with a sweet song, and finally stood before Hades and Persephone.

"How dare you invade my domains? If you do not provide a good reason, you will be doomed to suffer in Tartarus for eternity!" thundered Hades. With a lump in his throat, Orpheus replied: "I implore you to allow me to bring my beloved Eurydice back to the world of the living."

As Orpheus sang his request, the whole shadowy land stopped to listen. Sisyphus forgot his eternal torment, the furies halted in their torments, everyone was charmed by Orpheus. Even Hades was moved by his music and decided to grant him what he asked, on the condition that Orpheus would not look back at Eurydice during their return journey, otherwise he would lose her forever.

The couple set off through the dark passage that led back to the world of the living, with Orpheus leading the way and Eurydice behind him. But, just as daylight began to filter on the horizon, Orpheus, worried and impatient, couldn't resist and looked back. At that moment, Eurydice vanished, sucked back into the realm of the dead.

Orpheus, desperate, tried to go back to Hades, but Hermes stopped him, forcing him to return to the world of the living. From that day on, Orpheus lived in bitterness and solitude, his music was nothing but a lament of sadness. His story had a tragic ending: he was attacked and killed by a group of enraged Bacchantes, who did not tolerate his refusal.

But the legend of Orpheus does not end here. The Muses collected his divine lyre and his remains, and transformed them into a constellation, an eternal reminder in the starry sky. And, despite his sad end, it is said that Orpheus's spirit, once in the Elysian Fields, finally managed to embrace his beloved Eurydice again. Thus, in death, Orpheus and Eurydice found the eternal happiness that had been denied them in life.

Theseus and the Minotaur's Labyrinth

Upon his return to Athens, becoming the heir to the kingdom of Attica, Theseus faced a crisis. Emissaries from King Minos of Crete had arrived in Athens to collect the tribute due to the sovereign. Athens had been subjugated by Crete following a war sparked by the murder of Minos' son during a visit to the kingdom of Aegeus. According to the terms of the peace treaty, every year Athens had to send 14 youths as tribute to Crete: seven men and seven women.

Once they arrived in Crete, these young people were thrown into the terrifying labyrinth of Minos, where they became prey to the terrible Minotaur, a creature half-man, half-bull. The Athenians could no longer bear the idea of delivering their children as sacrificial victims, but they had no way to resist.

However, when Theseus learned of the situation, he decided to step in. He volunteered to be one of the young people delivered to Crete, promising that he would end the humiliation. He would travel with the other young people, but they would all return alive, having defeated the beast that fed on the blood of Athenian youth.

King Aegeus tried to dissuade Theseus from this idea, but to no avail. Watching his son set off, Aegeus blessed him, telling him that the ship that would carry him to Crete would hoist black sails, as a sign of mourning for the lives sacrificed. But if Theseus were to return safe and sound, he should hoist white sails. Thus, at the sight of the ship on the horizon, the king's heart would find immediate comfort.

Aegeus watched with anguish as the ship carrying his son disappeared over the horizon, not knowing if he would see him again. Once they arrived in Crete, the 14 youths were presented to King Minos. But during this ceremony, in the throne room, there was also the beautiful Princess Ariadne, who fell in love at first sight with handsome Theseus.

During the night, Ariadne secretly visited Theseus' cell, where he was awaiting his turn to be thrown into the labyrinth. She confessed her love for him and expressed her refusal to allow him to be killed by the horrible creature. Ariadne gave Theseus a sword and a ball of yarn. Theseus understood that the sword would allow him to defeat the monster, but he did not understand the purpose of the yarn. Ariadne explained that the yarn would show him the way out of the labyrinth.

The next day, Theseus entered the labyrinth with the other youths, leaving behind a trail of yarn. The labyrinth was dark and eerie, the air was tense and, at times, one could hear the snorts of the lurking creature. Bloodstains marred the ground and the labyrinth's walls, but Theseus, brave and determined, was set on not adding his own.

The Minotaur burst out suddenly, trying to kill Theseus. But our hero deftly avoided the beast's blows, and his counterattack was devastating. With a single blow, Theseus rid the world of the menacing presence of the Minotaur. Following the yarn trail left by Ariadne, Theseus and most of his companions managed to escape the labyrinth.

Outside, Ariadne was waiting for him, her eyes shiny with tears. They shared a passionate kiss before heading to the port, where the ship was ready to take them away from Crete. During the journey, the love between the two grew. But one night, Theseus was visited by the god Dionysus, who asked that their love story end. Ariadne was destined for the god of wine.

Out of respect for the gods, Theseus left Ariadne on the island of Naxos. The princess, heartbroken, saw the man she loved sail away. But she would not be left helpless, for she was destined for the god of ecstasy.

With a broken heart, Theseus resumed his journey to Athens. But in his sadness from the separation, he forgot to hoist the white sails, as he had promised his father. Aegeus, seeing the ship returning with black sails, threw himself from the cliff into the sea, overwhelmed by grief. From then on, those waters took the name of the Aegean Sea.

What was supposed to be a triumphant return turned into a melancholic one. Nevertheless, Theseus was hailed as a hero in Athens. He had killed the terrible Minotaur and was now the leader of Athens. His feats are inscribed in the stars, making him one of the most celebrated heroes of Greek mythology. His long reign was full of adventures and misfortunes, a true hero worthy of being remembered forever.

The Flight of Icarus

In ancient Athens, a city of art and wisdom, there resided Daedalus, an architect and inventor of such genius that his name echoed throughout all of Greece. Unfortunately, a tragic mistake forced Daedalus to abandon his birthplace, leaving behind the beauties he had created and seeking refuge elsewhere.

Daedalus found asylum on the island of Crete, ruled by the mighty King Minos, who enthusiastically welcomed the architect into his court. Daedalus worked for Minos, constructing extraordinary works such as the sumptuous palace of Knossos.

During this time, Daedalus fell deeply in love with an Egyptian slave. From their union, a son was born, Icarus. In the following years, Daedalus carried out his most notorious work: the labyrinth of Minos. A structure as vast as it was terrifying, designed to imprison the Minotaur, the monster half man and half bull.

However, in a cruel twist of fate, Daedalus and his young son Icarus were imprisoned in the very labyrinth that Daedalus himself had built. Accused of having helped the hero Theseus defeat the Minotaur, they were condemned to wander within the labyrinth. Daedalus was well aware that escape from Crete was impossible and, even if he had managed to escape, the island was heavily guarded both by land and by sea. Yet, Daedalus, with his ingenious inventiveness, conceived a daring and risky plan: to fly away from the island.

In the darkness of the labyrinth, Daedalus and Icarus began to collect pieces of wood and bird feathers. Daedalus's idea was to construct wings, light but sturdy, bound together by strips of beeswax.

After the construction was finished, Daedalus, his heart swelling with anxiety, fastened the wings onto his son's back, urging him, "Remember, Icarus, do not fly too close to the sea, for the dampness might ruin the wings, nor too high, otherwise, the sun could melt the wax. Stay close to me at all times."

Daedalus and Icarus climbed to the top of the highest tower of the labyrinth, and with a brave leap, they launched themselves into the open air. Flapping their wings like birds, they managed to soar into the sky and leave the island of Crete behind.

The world viewed from above was breathtakingly beautiful. But while Daedalus maintained a constant course, Icarus, ecstatic, flew with his eyes closed, penetrating among the clouds. He was completely intoxicated by the sensation of freedom and began to climb higher and higher, disregarding his father's warnings. Worried, Daedalus called out to his son, but the young boy failed to hear him.

His descent into tragedy was slow but inevitable. The wax wings, heated by the sun, began to melt. One by one, the feathers came loose, and Icarus started to fall. Daedalus, helpless, could only watch as his son plummeted towards the sea.

After a frantic search, Daedalus found Icarus's lifeless body on a deserted beach. That day, Daedalus understood the terrible price of his invention, his desire for freedom, a price he would have to pay for the rest of his life.

Atalanta and the Death Race

Atalanta was a little girl when her father, who desired only sons, abandoned her in a forest. This decision could have led her to a cruel fate, but instead, she was welcomed and raised by a bear along with two cubs. In her wild childhood, Atalanta developed a natural talent for hunting.

Her existence in the forest was disrupted when she was discovered by a group of hunters. Captivated by her skills, they decided to raise her and welcome her into their pack. Over time, Atalanta became a skilled hunter, joining the hunters who followed the goddess Artemis.

Her life took a turn when her father, filled with regrets for his wrongdoing, sought her out and asked for her forgiveness. Atalanta agreed and returned to her father's court, where she became famous for her speed, superior to that of a roe deer. Her reputation grew even further when she participated in the Calydonian Boar hunt, which tragically ended with the death of the brave Meleager.

However, a dark prophecy weighed on Atalanta: if she ever got married, her life would be ruined. Despite the prophecy, Atalanta, being breathtakingly beautiful and the daughter of a king, attracted many suitors. To protect her from the predicted fate, her father devised a plan: only he who defeated Atalanta in a race would have the right to marry her. In case of defeat, the suitor would pay with his life.

This warning did not discourage many aspiring suitors, who gambled their lives for Atalanta's hand, only to tragically lose the race. It seemed that Atalanta was safe until Hippomenes appeared, a young man of extraordinary speed. Atalanta had already met him in the past and knew he could run faster than her, but she also knew he wasn't able to maintain that speed for long.

To win Atalanta's heart, Hippomenes sought the help of the goddess of love, Aphrodite. The goddess provided him with golden apples and instructions on how to use them during the race. During the race, every time Atalanta was about to overtake him, Hippomenes would throw a golden apple. Atalanta, distracted by the beauty of the fruit, slowed down to pick it up, allowing Hippomenes to maintain the advantage and ultimately win.

Atalanta's father, happy that the prophecy had been avoided, gave his daughter in marriage to Hippomenes. The couple got married and, seemingly, everything seemed fine. However, in an act of neglected gratitude, they forgot to thank Aphrodite.

The goddess, annoyed by the couple's ingratitude, decided to punish them. She unleashed an uncontrollable passion in them, which culminated in a love encounter inside the temple dedicated to Rhea, the mother of Zeus. Irritated by this lack of respect, Rhea transformed Atalanta and Hippomenes into lions.

For additional punishment, they were condemned to pull Rhea's chariot, eternally serving the mother of the Olympian gods. Thus ends the story of Atalanta, a reminder of both the strength of human will and the necessity of respecting the gods.

The Hand of Midas

In the distant Kingdom of Phrygia, the wine-loving God, Dionysus, found himself in quite a pickle. He was unable to find his faithful drinking companion, Silenus, who was also his precious mentor and adoptive father. Silenus was a renowned sage, known for offering his deepest lessons while in a state of inebriation, and he had the gift of prophecy.

One day, Silenus was discovered passed out in a forest by the local farmers, having succumbed to an excess of drink. Recognizing him, they took him to King Midas, who warmly welcomed him into his palace. For days, Midas's court celebrated the illustrious guest with banquets and drinks.

When Dionysus discovered that his old friend had been so generously welcomed, he decided to thank King Midas by offering him a wish of his choice. Midas, driven by ambition, immediately expressed his wish: "I want everything I touch to turn into gold." Dionysus, concerned about the king's hasty choice, tried to make him reflect: "Are you sure?". But Midas answered confidently: "Yes, indeed, I will be the richest man who has ever lived."

Dionysus granted Midas's wish, but felt a strong regret for the king's ill-considered choice. Midas, eager to test his new power, picked up a small stone that lay on the ground and it immediately turned into pure gold. Full of euphoria, Midas touched several things that, without exception, all turned into gold.

Midas's euphoria soon turned into terror when he tried to eat an apple. As soon as his finger brushed the fruit, it turned into a solid block of gold. Midas tried a new approach and grabbed a fork, which immediately turned into gold, and tried to stick it into a piece of bread. But the bread too turned into gold, and the king broke a tooth in an attempt to bite it.

The realization of disaster made its way into Midas's mind. What he had thought was a divine gift turned out to be a terrible curse. Midas felt his end was inevitable, as he would quickly die of starvation and he collapsed in tears on the dining table. The king's daughter, seeing her father in this state, tried to comfort him and touched his hand. She immediately turned into a gold statue.

Midas, desperate, turned to Dionysus, begging him to revoke the terrible power. Dionysus, moved by the king's despair, indicated how to free himself from the curse. He had to immerse himself in the waters of the Pactolus River and, once in the water, pray that the power of his touch be removed.

Midas followed Dionysus's instructions. As soon as he immersed himself in the water, the sand on the riverbed turned into grains of pure gold and the scales of the fish began to shine like gold. But when he came out of the water, Midas discovered that the curse was finally lifted. Everything he touched returned to normal, including his daughter.

After this painful experience, Midas renounced all forms of wealth and retreated to live a simple, humble life in the fields and forests, in the company of the God Pan.

Eco and Narcissus

Once upon a time, in the lush and verdant Greece, lived an extraordinarily beautiful nymph named Echo. Echo was known for her vivacity and joy of life. She was always ready to play in the meadows, dance among the trees, and accompany Artemis, the goddess of the hunt, in her adventures. However, Echo had a small flaw: she was a great chatterbox and loved to have the last word in every conversation.

This little flaw proved to be her downfall when Zeus, the lord of Olympus, began to visit the nymphs on his travels on earth. One day, suspecting her husband's adventures, Zeus's wife, Hera, descended to earth to look for him. Seeing Hera approaching, Echo tried to distract her, speaking non-stop and flattering the goddess with compliments about her beauty. All this, however, was just to give Zeus time to escape.

Hera, however, was not a goddess to be trifled with. She soon discovered Echo's deception and decided to punish her. She took away her voice, leaving her only the ability to repeat the last word of what others said. Echo was forced to wander in the woods, unable to express her thoughts and emotions.

One day, during her walks in the woods, she crossed paths with the beautiful Narcissus. Instantly, her heart caught fire for him, but she was condemned to silence, able to only repeat the last words she heard.

Narcissus was a young man of extraordinary beauty, famous throughout Greece for his charm and his disdain for others' affections. One day, during a hunting trip with his companions, he got lost in the thick of the woods. As he searched for his way back, he heard a rustle coming from a bush and cautiously asked, "Is anyone there?". And Echo's voice replied, "There... there... there...".

Attracted by the sound, Narcissus approached the nymph and she, overwhelmed by passion, tried to touch him. However, he pushed her away roughly and said, "Leave me, I don't want you". Poor Echo, all she could say was, "I want you... I want you...". Narcissus, frightened, ran away, leaving Echo alone with her broken heart.

As she wandered in the woods, Echo came across a group of nymphs, who were also rejected by Narcissus. But unlike Echo, they were not ready to accept their fate. They therefore cried out to Nemesis, the goddess of revenge, asking her to punish Narcissus for his arrogant behavior. Nemesis, listening to their prayers, decided to punish Narcissus by teaching him a hard lesson about unrequited love.

During one of his walks, Narcissus stopped at a spring to quench his thirst. As he lowered himself to drink, he saw his reflection in the water and was immediately captivated by his own beauty. He tried to touch the reflected image, but when he did, the reflection vanished. Narcissus, obsessed with his image, lamented, "Why do you flee from me? You smile at me, then you scorn me?".

Echo, who was watching from afar, witnessed the poignant scene. Narcissus, now neglecting himself, spent his days contemplating his reflection in the water, refusing to eat or drink. So obsessed with his image, Narcissus ended up falling into the water in an attempt to reach his reflection. Too weak to resurface, he drowned.

His spirit was led to the world of the dead, where he continued to contemplate his image in the waters of the River Acheron during his journey. In the place where his body was buried, a flower of rare beauty grew, which the nymphs decided to call "Narcissus".

Echo, meanwhile, was overwhelmed by grief. She decided to retreat into a mountain cave, far from the world she once knew. As time passed, she merged with the mountain. But even today, if you call Echo, you can hear her respond, ready to repeat the last word.

Perseus and Medusa

The valiant Perseus undertook a daring mission: to hunt and defeat the feared Gorgon Medusa. His journey led him on an adventure across the boundless lands of Greece, in search of any clue that could reveal Medusa's hideout. Despite his efforts, his progress seemed slow and fruitless. But Fortune, capricious as ever, decided to favor him, and the gods decided to intervene.

The messenger of the gods, Hermes, appeared to Perseus to offer his guidance. Revealing to him that brute force and courage alone would not overcome the Gorgon, Hermes suggested that Perseus should arm himself with special tools. Such objects were under the custody of the Nymphs of the North, mystical creatures whose location was a secret known only to the Graeae, three gray witches endowed with a single shared eye. Thanks to his knowledge of all paths, Hermes guided Perseus to the dwelling of the Graeae.

Before Perseus could set off, Hermes gave him a divine sword, forged with masterful skill in the forges of Hephaestus. This magnificent weapon, with its perpetually sharp edge, would play a crucial role in Perseus's destiny. With such a gift in hand, Perseus ventured into the hideout of the Graeae. Taking advantage of a moment of passage of the single eye among the witches, Perseus managed to seize it.

Without their eye, the Graeae found themselves powerless and begged Perseus to return it. The hero, as cunning as he was brave, proposed a deal: he would return the eye only if the witches revealed the location of the Nymphs of the North. In the absence of alternatives, the Graeae accepted, allowing Perseus to continue his journey.

The Nymphs of the North lived in the idyllic country of the Hyperboreans, a place where the sun shone eternally. They welcomed him with generosity, reserved only for the sons of Zeus, and gave him the gifts he needed: winged sandals similar to those of Hermes, the sacred helmet of Hades which conferred invisibility, and a magic bag to contain his precious trophy.

The goddess Athena, Perseus's half-sister, gave him a gift of incalculable value: her splendid shield, the Aegis, which once belonged to Zeus. Now, armed to the teeth, Perseus was ready for the final confrontation with Medusa.

Reaching the Gorgon's lair, Perseus was greeted by a series of stone statues, silent witnesses to the deadly power of Medusa's gaze. Wearing Hades' helmet, Perseus managed to pass unnoticed by the other two Gorgons, Stheno and Euryale, who were guarding the entrance.

The presence of the hero did not go unnoticed to Medusa, but without being able to see the intruder, the monster remained waiting. Knowing the danger that the Gorgon's gaze represented, Perseus advanced with extreme caution, keeping his eyes closed and using the sounds of the snakes on Medusa's head as a guide. However, a fortuitous error revealed his position to Medusa, who launched an arrow at him. Thanks to his prodigious reflexes, Perseus managed to block the shot with his shield, and in the act, a brilliant idea flashed to him.

Using the reflection of the shield as a mirror, Perseus was able to observe Medusa without looking directly into her petrifying face. This cunning allowed him to strike a lethal blow to the creature, beheading her. The terrible monster had been defeated, and her head was promptly stowed away in the magic bag.

From the Gorgon's spilled blood, two new creatures arose: the giant Chrysaor with his golden sword, and the magnificent winged horse Pegasus, the fruit of the union between Poseidon and Medusa.

Perseus, with his trophy in hand, took flight thanks to his winged sandals, pointing to his homeland. But the road home would still be full of challenges. However, with courage in his heart and divine gifts at his disposal, Perseus was ready to face any headwind he might encounter.

Bellerophon

In the ancient city of Corinth, the descendants of Sisyphus, the man known for even tricking the gods, held power. The king, Glaucus, had two sons: Deliades, his favorite, and Bellerophon, so handsome that people whispered that he was a descendant of Poseidon. However, despite Bellerophon's beauty, the rivalry between the two brothers was undeniable. Every time they practiced their martial arts, Bellerophon was defeated.

But, like a grain of sand becoming a pearl, Bellerophon progressed, growing in strength and agility. The clashes between the two became more violent, the competition sharpening with each new fight. Even though Bellerophon was constantly improving, Deliades maintained an advantage.

In the heart of the fight, Deliades displayed an almost unbearable arrogance, challenging his brother to make mistakes. But Bellerophon, fueled by frustration, unleashed his fury in an epic battle. Fatigue was forgotten, and he managed to defeat Deliades. In a swift move, Bellerophon managed to hit the prince's head with such force that he fell to the ground.

Paralyzed by the sight of his brother inert, Bellerophon rushed to his aid. But it was too late: the young prince's soul was already heading towards Hades' kingdom.

The king, horrified by the tragedy, arrived just in time to see Bellerophon with his brother in his arms, in the deepest grief. The king's heart, already broken by the loss of his favorite son, made a painful decision. He banished Bellerophon from his kingdom, ordering him never to return.

The young prince left Corinth under the reproachful eyes of his fellow citizens, who harbored a deep affection for the late Deliades. The weight of remorse and punishment bore heavily on Bellerophon's shoulders as he crossed the boundaries of his hometown.

Aimless, Bellerophon wandered through Greece until he reached Tiryns, a city ruled by King Proetus. Upon learning that the exiled son of the king of Corinth was on his land, Proetus offered him refuge, respecting the ancient law of hospitality imposed by Zeus. Bellerophon told the king the tragic story of his exile, emphasizing that it was all a terrible accident. Deeply moved, Proetus promised to help him.

The king organized a purification ritual to atone for the Corinthian prince's sins. Thanks to the sacrifices to the gods, Bellerophon's sins were washed away. Now free from his sins but burdened with gratitude, Bellerophon looked to the future with renewed hope.

Queen Antea of Tiryns could not hide her admiration for young Bellerophon. His beauty and strength, now at their peak, had generated an intense desire in the queen's heart. However, Bellerophon did not seem to notice. One day, invited to a private meeting with the queen, he found himself facing woman-made temptation.

Antea, exploiting all her seductive beauty, tried to attract him. But Bellerophon, faithful and grateful to his host, did not even conceive of committing such a betrayal and rejected the queen's advances.

Antea, indignant and humiliated, hurled furious insults at the Corinthian prince, questioning his virility. Bellerophon, however, ignored her and left, leaving her to rant on her knees. The queen, however, was not willing to endure such an affront and decided to take revenge.

With fake tears streaming down her face, Antea told her husband a false rape attempt by Bellerophon. The king, filled with a wave of anger, would have wanted to attack the young man, but the sacred duty of hospitality imposed by Zeus prevented him. Despite this, Proetus was a cunning man and conceived a plan to get rid of the guest he believed had dishonored his house.

He had the scribe write a letter to his father-in-law and entrusted Bellerophon with the task of delivering it to Iobates, the king of Lycia. Bellerophon naively accepted the task, grateful to his host, unaware of the sinister intentions behind the apparent request.

Arriving at the Lycian court, Bellerophon was warmly welcomed by King Iobates, who refused to read the letter before offering the visitor a taste of his hospitality. During a grand feast, Iobates introduced the young prince to his splendid daughter, immediately igniting in Bellerophon's soul the arrows of Eros.

Struggling to regain his composure, Bellerophon finally delivers the message to the King. Iobates, astonished by the content of the letter, finds out that the guest had tried to violate his own daughter and deserved suitable punishment.

Although furious, Iobates noticed Bellerophon's sincere interest in his daughter. Seeing the opportunity to rid himself of the young prince, he proposed a mission to Bellerophon: he would give his daughter's hand if

Bellerophon could rid the kingdom of a terrible creature that was sowing destruction.

Iobates described the creature as a scourge on his kingdom: villages destroyed, crops burned, livestock wiped out. All this devastation had been caused by a monster called Chimera, a terrifying creature descended from Typhon and Echidna, two of the most formidable creatures in the Greek world. The Chimera had a lion's head, a goat's head, and a snake's tail. Its strength was devastating, and its fiery breath destroyed everything it touched.

Bellerophon, his heart swollen with courage and love, immediately accepted the challenge and set off to confront the fearsome creature, oblivious to Iobates' real intentions. The king of Lycia, in fact, waited with some satisfaction for Bellerophon, the man he suspected had attempted to dishonor his daughter, to venture towards a seemingly fatal destiny.

Before the encounter with the evil creature, a divine surprise changed the course of events. Bellerophon, at a crucial turning point in his destiny, came across the magnificent winged horse Pegasus. Born from the union of Medusa and Poseidon, Pegasus suddenly appeared in front of him, drinking water from a stream. Bellerophon understood that if he could tame this creature, he would have an unstoppable force.

Approaching stealthily, Bellerophon jumped on the winged animal. Pegasus, startled, reacted frantically and unseated the audacious young man who fell to the ground, hitting his head on a rock. Thus, Bellerophon fell into a deep sleep, his mind wandering in the Realm of Morpheus, the God of dreams.

In his sleep, a vision of Athena, the goddess of wisdom, appeared. She held golden reins in her hand. With a gentle smile, she passed the magic reins to Bellerophon, whom she was very fond of, and revealed the secret to taming Pegasus.

When Bellerophon awoke, the divine reins were in his hands and Pegasus was still there, waiting patiently. Following the instructions he received in his dream, the hero approached the majestic steed and gently placed the reins on it. The Corinthian prince mounted the winged horse and together they began to gallop. The harmony between rider and horse was so complete that together they took flight, piercing the clouds as if they were a single entity.

From up there, Bellerophon spotted a huge column of smoke, an unmistakable sign of the presence of the Chimera, the terrible beast that had destroyed everything in its path, reducing the village to a heap of flames.

Bellerophon carefully analyzed his prey. The beast was more dangerous than he imagined, spitting fire at the hero, but the winged steed was able to agilely avoid the attacks. Flying in a circle around the Chimera, Bellerophon and Pegasus confused it more and more.

When the time to attack came, the Chimera lunged at Pegasus, but the animal responded with a hoof blow to the beast's head. Bellerophon, seeing the opportunity, jumped from his horse and pierced the Chimera with his lance. The beast was dead. Overwhelmed by a wave of power, Bellerophon found himself believing the rumors that said he was Poseidon's son.

Bellerophon returned to Iobates' palace with the head of the Chimera as a trophy. The king was impressed, not expecting the young man to be able to achieve such a daunting task. Promising Bellerophon the princess's hand only after neutralizing two other threats - the Solymi and the Amazons - Iobates broke his word.

Despite the disappointment, the hero accepted these new tasks out of love for the princess. He confronted and defeated the Solymi, wild warriors sons of Ares, and not even the Amazons managed to stop him. He returned to Lycia bringing with him the heads of the marauders who had terrorized the kingdom.

Finally understanding that Bellerophon was a man blessed by the gods and that he had been victimized by unfounded rumors, Iobates accepted him as his son-in-law and named him his heir. Bellerophon had achieved everything a man could desire: a beautiful family, the governance of Lycia in place of his father-in-law. But the desire for glory pushed him to want more.

In a burst of pride, he mounted Pegasus and flew towards Olympus, believing he deserved a place among the gods. This presumption did not go unnoticed. Zeus, king of the gods, shaken by such audacity and insolent arrogance, sent a gadfly to sting Pegasus. Frightened, the winged horse unseated Bellerophon who plummeted to the earth.

Some tell that Bellerophon met a terrible end, others that he was saved by Athena and spent the rest of his life trying to find Pegasus again. What is certain, however, is that he never managed to find his faithful steed. Pegasus, in fact, became immortal at the will of the gods and was placed among the stars.

The Apple of Discord

In the heart of the lush, verdant countryside, a young shepherd named Paris tended to his flock. One day, he noticed, with surprise, that one of his calves, seized by a mysterious curiosity, was venturing towards a solitary cave. Concerned, Paris decided to follow it, unaware that he was soon to become the protagonist of an event that would change the course of history.

Inside the cave, he didn't find the lost calf, but instead, was greeted by an awe-inspiring sight: three women of such extraordinary beauty that they seemed divine. Entranced by their grace, Paris immediately recognized that he was in the presence of goddesses.

On the same day, far from there, the Nereid Thetis and the hero Peleus were united in a lavish celebration to which all the deities of Olympus had been invited. The atmosphere was cheerful and vibrant, with the gods celebrating around a sumptuous banquet. However, a shadow had fallen on the event: Eris, the goddess of discord, had not been invited.

Infuriated by the slight, Eris decided to exact her revenge. As Athena, the goddess of wisdom, Aphrodite, the goddess of love, and Hera, the queen of the gods, chatted amicably at the banquet table, Eris soared above them and threw a golden apple of stunning beauty among the three goddesses. Engraved on the shining surface of the fruit was the phrase "To the fairest". This marked the beginning of the dispute for the "Apple of Discord".

The three goddesses, each convinced of their own superiority, began to contest the apple. But Zeus, the king of the gods, intervened with a mighty roar, halted the dispute, and decided to resolve the dilemma by appointing an impartial judge. In a world populated by millions of men, fate chose Paris.

He wasn't the wisest, nor a profound scholar of the concept of justice, but the Moirai, the weavers of destiny, had spun this path for him. Hermes, the messenger of the gods, delivered the apple to Paris, explaining his mission. Three goddesses presented themselves to him, each offering him a gift in exchange for the golden apple.

Hera promised him riches and a palace as splendid as Olympus, while Athena offered wisdom and the chance to become the world's greatest general. Lastly, Aphrodite, the goddess of love and beauty, promised him the love of the most beautiful of mortals: Helen of Sparta.

Struck by Helen's beauty, Paris was unable to resist Aphrodite's offer. He handed the golden apple to the goddess of love, thus consecrating her victory. Aphrodite rejoiced, but the seed of bitterness and resentment had been planted in the hearts of Athena and Hera.

Paris' act would unleash their vengeance, condemning the Trojan prince and his people to a fate of pain and destruction. But of this, the young shepherd knew nothing. At least, not yet.

Hercules and the Nemean Lion

Hercules, powerful and valiant, had offered to serve his cousin Eurystheus, who was the king of Mycenae at the time. However, Eurystheus harbored suspicions about his cousin, fearing that he might aspire to the throne, given his extraordinary strength. To ward off such a threat, Eurystheus decided to test Hercules by assigning him an apparently insurmountable task: he was to defeat a gigantic lion that was spreading terror in the forests of Argolis.

The fierce beast, offspring of the fearsome Typhon and the malicious Echidna, had taken the liberty of attacking the herds of the region and, after tasting human flesh, seemed to have developed a particular preference for it. Legend had it that its skin was resistant to any traditional weapon, making Hercules' task even more difficult. Despite this, armed with his trusted bow, arrows, and club, Hercules decided to accept the challenge.

Hercules spent a period of time in the dense forests of Nemea, searching for any clue that could lead him to the lion's den. In the end, his efforts were rewarded when he was able to locate traces that led him directly to the beast's dwelling. The cave was a gloomy and dark place, filled with animal bones and human skulls, an unmistakable clue to the lion's passage.

The demigod, brave and determined, entered the lion's lair. Despite the heavy breathing of the monster echoing throughout the cave, Hercules was not shaken. When the lion appeared, it let out a roar so powerful that it would make the heart of mortals tremble, but Hercules was no ordinary man; Zeus's blood flowed in his veins.

Without hesitation, Hercules fired an arrow at the lion, but it bounced off its leathery skin without causing any damage. The lion, enraged, lunged at Hercules, initiating a fierce battle. Despite the powerful blows inflicted with his club, Hercules could not hurt the beast. Realizing the futility of his weapons, he decided to grapple with the lion in hand-to-hand combat.

In an epic clash, the lion drove its sharp claws into Hercules' body, causing excruciating pain. However, the hero, with superhuman strength, wrapped his arms around the lion's neck, squeezing with all his might. The monster could not resist Hercules' grip and eventually died, suffocated by the hero's strength.

With great satisfaction, Hercules used the beast's claws to skin it, then donned its hide as a trophy of his triumph. Upon his return to Mycenae, the fearful Eurystheus fled at the sight of Hercules, fearing his wrath and hiding in a vat.

And so, Hercules completed his first labor, taking a significant step towards glory.

Hercules and the Invincible Hydra of Lerna

For his second labor, the heroic Hercules received a command from King Eurystheus to confront a terrifying monster residing in the region of Lerna. This creature, offspring of Typhon and Echidna, was the horrific Hydra. In this daunting challenge, Hercules wasn't alone; by his side was his loyal nephew Iolaus, who had been his companion since their youth.

Their journey led them through a village devastated by the creature. A survivor managed to point them in the direction of the monster's lair. The Hydra had chosen the dark swamps surrounding Lerna as its home. So, Hercules and Iolaus ventured into the fetid air of the swamp in search of the beast's hideout.

Hidden within a cave, the Hydra was lured out from the shadows by a flaming arrow shot from Hercules' mighty bow. The sight of the Hydra was dreadful: a monster with many heads, each of which emitted a roar that shook the ground.

Despite his formidable stature, Hercules proved agile, deftly avoiding the beast's attacks. With a powerful swing of his club, he crushed one of the monster's heads, only to discover with horror that two more immediately sprouted in its place.

Thus began an epic battle, in which Hercules beheaded the Hydra's heads with his sword, only to see them double in number. Seeing the futility of this tactic, Iolaus shouted for Hercules to stop. Then, he had a revelation: as Hercules severed the heads, Iolaus cauterized the wounds with a fire torch, thus preventing their regeneration.

One by one, the Hydra's heads fell. The goddess Hera, an enemy of Hercules, sent giant crabs to aid the Hydra, but they only managed to distract the hero briefly and were soon crushed under his powerful foot. Hercules and Iolaus finally defeated the Hydra's last head, and though the creature was still alive, it was now helpless. Hercules then threw it into a pit and buried it under a massive stone.

The Hydra's blood was known for its deadly toxicity, and exploiting this knowledge, Hercules dipped his arrows in the monster's blood, thus acquiring a terribly powerful weapon.

Victorious, Hercules and Iolaus returned to Mycenae. Hera, in her spite, honored the creatures that had fought for her, immortalizing them in the sky through the constellation of Cancer.

The Great Duel between Hector and Achilles

For almost a decade on the battlefield, men and gods eagerly anticipated the clash of the two greatest warriors of the Trojan War. Achilles, the champion of the Greeks, was consumed by uncontrollable wrath, eager to avenge the death of his dear friend Patroclus. On the other side, Hector, the most valiant among the Trojans, fought to protect his homeland, his people, and his family.

Achilles' eyes burned with hatred for his opponent. Though invisible to human eyes, Phobos, the personification of fear, was by his side. Hector's heart was filled with fear, and his survival instinct urged him to flee. From the walls of Troy, King Priam, his wife Hecuba, and the princes watched anxiously. Hector, pursued by Achilles, acted like a prey chased by a ravenous predator.

Hector dodged arrows and javelins thrown by warriors following Achilles. The son of Peleus ordered his men to stop attacking the Trojan prince because it was his intent to send Hector's spirit to Hades. At this point, Zeus decided that it was time to weigh Hector's fate on his golden scale. Achilles' plate rose towards glory, while Hector's sank towards Hades. Hector's fate had been decided by the gods.

Zeus ordered Athena to descend to earth and ensure that the warrior's fate, as set by the Moirai, was respected. Athena whispered in Achilles' ear, telling him to stop chasing his enemy and encourage him to fight. Hector then heard the voice of Prince Deiphobus and was relieved to see his brother by his side in his hour of need.

The Trojan prince finally found the courage to face the Achaean champion. He tried to reach an agreement with Achilles: the fallen warrior's body would be returned to his comrades to receive due honors and funeral rites. But Achilles refused, claiming there could be no agreement between lions and men and that it was the will of the gods to grant him victory. He would throw the prince's body to the dogs.

The two greatest warriors faced off in front of the imposing gates of Troy, while citizens watched breathlessly from the top of the walls. This clash could have changed the outcome of the war.

Hector hurled his spear at Achilles, but the son of Peleus easily dodged it thanks to the divine armor given to him by Hephaestus. Hector asked his brother for another spear, but Deiphobus was absent: he realized that he had been tricked by the gods and that Athena had disguised herself as his brother to spur him on. Despite knowing that the gods were not on his side, this time Hector did not let himself be overcome by fear. He drew his sword and rushed forward to meet his fate. On the walls, the king and queen feared for the life of their beloved son and for the fate of their kingdom, should Hector fall.

Hector bravely fought against the most powerful warrior in the world. The two heroes lunged at each other in a duel that seemed like a deadly ballet. Within moments of the start of the clash, Achilles had already understood how Hector behaved in battle. No blow from the enemy could reach him and now he was just waiting for the prince to reveal a vulnerable point to decide the outcome of the fight.

Hector stepped forward against the son of Peleus, but with a perfect blow, Achilles fatally cut Hector's neck. The great duel was over.

Cries of pain and despair rose from the city walls and everyone mourned the death of the noblest of the Trojans. Princess Andromache, Hector's wife, fainted when she learned that her husband had died and that little

Astyanax was now an orphan.

With the spear still lodged in his neck, Hector begged Achilles to hand over his body to his parents in exchange for a rich ransom in gold. But the ruthless Achilles refused. Hector's body was to be eaten by the dogs and vultures that roamed the Greek camp.

With his last breath, Hector cursed Achilles and swore that the god Apollo would avenge him. But Achilles replied that he did not fear meeting Thanatos, for he had already fulfilled his destiny by killing the best of the Trojans and his name would be remembered for centuries to come.

Hector's spirit set off for Hades, but his body was still to suffer many humiliations. Achilles tied the prince's ankles with a rope and attached it to his chariot. He then dragged Hector's body around the city of Troy, showing every inhabitant that their champion was dead and that all hope for Troy was gone.

Priam, seeing his son's body dragged before the walls, tried to throw himself from the top to take his own life, but was held back by his sons. Meanwhile, Hecuba, the queen, screamed and tore her hair.

Achilles dragged Hector's body into the Greek camp and wherever he went he was greeted by Greek warriors cheering his victory. After achieving his revenge, Achilles was finally ready to give Patroclus a worthy burial.

The Trojan Horse

After a decade of grueling war, in the heart of the night, Trojan sentinels observed a mysterious glow lighting up the sky above the Greek camp. Columns of smoke rose, indicating something extraordinary was happening.

The dawn of the following day brought a stunning discovery. The Greek camp had been abandoned, the Achaean warriors had vanished, and in the midst of desolation, a giant wooden horse stood. This monumental equine, built with the abandoned Greek ships, seemed like a tribute to the gods.

In the confusion, the Trojans found a Greek man, Sinon, whipped and tied to a post. The man told of being left as a sacrifice, a tribute to placate the gods and ensure a safe return home for the Greeks.

Questioned about the mysterious departure of the Greeks after a decade-long siege, Sinon revealed that the Greeks had aroused the wrath of the goddess Athena, offended by the theft of the Palladium from her temple in Troy. This insult had brought a great pestilence among the Achaeans, making them understand the impossibility of conquering Troy without divine aid. And so, they decided to withdraw.

The giant horse, Sinon said, was an offering to the goddess. Its grandeur was designed to prevent the Trojans from bringing it into the city, as the gods would surely favor whoever possessed such a tribute.

King Priam, his nobles, and priests were faced with a difficult decision. Some proposed to burn the horse, but this would surely trigger the wrath of the gods. Others suggested leaving it where it was. However, the idea of bringing this tribute to the gods within the city of Troy was too tempting to resist.

Cassandra, the unfortunate and despised prophetess, pleaded with the Trojans to destroy that cursed monument, but her words fell on deaf ears, as had already happened years ago when she predicted the defeat of Troy.

What the Trojans did not know was that inside the horse hid the most valiant Greek warriors. Among them were Odysseus, Menelaus, Diomedes, Pyrrhus, and Epeus, the skilled carpenter who had built the gigantic horse.

After a monumental effort, the horse was dragged inside the city walls. The great gate was partially demolished to let the enormous structure through. Meanwhile, hidden in a nearby cove, the great Greek army impatiently waited for the signal to attack.

Once the horse was positioned at the center of the temple square, the whole city burst into celebrations. They toasted to the victory over the

Greeks after ten long years of war. The night advanced, and the city fell into deep silence.

Suddenly, a hatch opened in the belly of the wooden horse. From there, dozens of Greek warriors emerged, quietly infiltrating the deserted streets. They took control of the city gates, surprising the sentinels. A signal fire was launched, and thousands of Greek warriors, led by Agamemnon, invaded the city, initiating a bloodbath.

Neither the young nor women were spared. The bloodthirsty fury of the Achaeans seemed unstoppable. Many Trojan men tried to resist, but the fate of Troy was now sealed.

The final assault on the Royal Palace, led by the son of Achilles, marked the end of Trojan resistance. The Trojan War was reaching its tragic conclusion.

Achilles' Heel

As dawn painted the sky with shades of red and gold, Achilles, the indomitable Greek warrior, led the final assault against the solid walls of Troy. The city, a symbol of power and resistance, seemed within reach, and victory was now a mere breath away. Using long ladders, the audacious Achaeans attempted to scale the Trojan walls. The defenders, with their courage tested, responded with desperate resistance. It was Aeneas, the proud son of Aphrodite, who led the Trojans out from the walls. Had they failed to destroy the great ladder, the city would have been irretrievably lost.

Yet Achilles, with his untamed fury, continued to claim victims among the Trojans. Seeing the power of Achilles, the defenders' courage began to waver. Realizing imminent death, many Trojans fled, only to be pierced by the ruthless spear of Peleus in Achilles' hands.

At that very moment, Apollo, the Sun God, appeared to Achilles. He ordered him to halt his advance, for his destiny had already been written: he was never meant to breach the walls of Troy. But Achilles, proud and indomitable, ignored the divine warning. He dared to challenge Apollo, even threatening to strike him with his spear.

Achilles' presumption did not go unnoticed. Apollo guided Prince Paris to fire an arrow against the powerful Greek warrior. With a surprising skill in archery, and with Apollo's assistance, Paris launched an arrow that struck Achilles' heel, his only weak point.

Legend has it that Achilles was almost invincible since his mother, the goddess Thetis, had dipped him into the waters of the Styx River as a child. The only part of his body that had not been bathed - and therefore the only vulnerable one - was his heel.

As blood soaked the earth beneath him, Achilles was mortally wounded. The Greek colossus, despite the pain, rose with his last strength and managed to deliver a few final, devastating blows. But the wound was too severe. With a thunderous sound that echoed across the battlefield, Achilles fell. The greatest hero had been defeated.

Ajax, another brave Greek warrior, reached Achilles' body to protect it from the Trojans trying to loot his armor. While Ajax defended the hero's corpse, Odysseus provided cover for strong Ajax to hoist Achilles' body onto his shoulders and head for the Greek camp.

Exhausted but determined, Ajax managed to complete his mission and return his friend's body to the Greek camp. There, Achilles' body received due honors, and the Achaean warriors mourned the death of the greatest among them.

Thetis, Achilles' mother, emerged from the sea to bid her son farewell one last time. Her tears flowed onto her son's body as all bystanders watched, moved by the heartbreaking scene. In the end, Achilles was cremated on a funeral pyre worthy of a king. His bones were buried next to the remains of his beloved friend Patroclus. Finally, the two friends would meet again in the Elysian Fields.

Ulysses on the Island of the Cyclopes

Ulysses and his comrades had spent countless days at sea, engaged in their heroic attempt to return home, when they finally discovered land on the horizon. It was the notorious island of the Cyclopes, single-eyed creatures, offspring of Poseidon, the powerful god of the seas. Ulysses, driven by a natural curiosity and an indomitable spirit of adventure, selected twelve of his bravest men to explore the island with him.

Faced with a gigantic cave, from which the agitated bleating of sheep came, they decided to enter. Inside, they realized that this place was the dwelling of one of the fearsome inhabitants of the island. In the cave there was a pen with sheep, amphoras full of goat milk and bowls overflowing with fresh cheese. Ulysses tasted a bit of that cheese, and was about to steal it, but decided to wait for the return of the owner of the cave and negotiate with him. But he would soon regret that decision.

The huge cyclops appeared in front of the cave entrance, bringing with him part of his herd that he had led to graze. Ulysses and his men hid, scared, but their presence was revealed when the cyclops lit a fire in the center of the cave. Ulysses stepped forward and, with courage bordering on audacity, introduced himself to the monster, explaining the reason for his presence and invoking hospitality. The cyclops replied that his name was Polyphemus, the proudest of his race, and that he did not recognize the laws of men, so he had no obligation of hospitality.

Polyphemus, with a frightful gesture, grabbed two of Ulysses' men by the legs and slammed them to the ground, killing them on the spot. And if that was not enough, the creature devoured them completely. Then, with an equally terrifying gesture, he moved a huge boulder and blocked the cave's exit. Ulysses thought to take advantage of the cyclops' sleep to kill him, but soon realized that it would be impossible to remove the heavy rock that blocked the exit.

The next day, the giant went out to lead his sheep to pasture, leaving the sailors trapped in the cave. Ulysses, seizing this opportunity, concocted a plan for revenge. He found a large tree trunk and sharpened one end. At the end of the day, the cyclops returned and, after entering, closed the cave exit again with the boulder. Ulysses then offered Polyphemus a jar full of his men's finest wine. The cyclops drank the wine offered by Ulysses with gusto and appreciated the gesture, even promising that

Ulysses would be the last to be devoured. Curious, he asked Ulysses' name, who replied, "Nobody."

After drinking, the mighty Polyphemus, drunk, fell asleep. This was the moment Ulysses was waiting for. He took the sharpened tree trunk and, with his men, rushed at the cyclops' single eye, piercing it. The cyclops woke up screaming in pain. At the sound of his screams, other cyclopes approached the cave and asked who had hurt him. Polyphemus shouted, "Nobody! Nobody has blinded me!". Since there was no one to punish, they returned to their homes.

The next day, Polyphemus let the sheep out to graze, not imagining that Ulysses had another ace up his sleeve. By attaching themselves to the bellies of the stoutest rams, Ulysses and his men managed to elude the cyclops' surveillance and escape from his cave. Once outside, they ran to their ships and sailed quickly.

Ulysses, once aboard, could not restrain himself and shouted at the monster that his blindness was a just punishment for violating the laws of divine hospitality. Polyphemus, furious, ripped a huge piece of rock from a mountain and threw it at Ulysses. The rock fell near the ship, shaking it violently. Ulysses' men begged him to stop provoking the cyclops, but Ulysses did not listen. He proudly claimed his victory, revealing to the cyclops his real name, Ulysses, the destroyer of Troy, son of Laertes, the king of Ithaca.

The cyclops, furious, threw another boulder that grazed the ship. Ulysses and his men managed to escape, with the regret of having lost some comrades, but also with the excitement of having overcome a terrible test. Polyphemus, however, did not give up so easily and asked his father Poseidon to punish Ulysses, preventing him from returning home. His wish would be granted: Ulysses would wander for years before returning to Ithaca, without a ship, without treasures, and without companions. His pride would have a very high price, as he now had against him the powerful god of the seas, Poseidon.

CHAPTER 6

Interpreting the myths through Ancient Greek society values

In this chapter, we will explore how these ancient legends reflect the values, aspirations, and fears of one of the most influential civilizations of antiquity. Myths are not just fascinating tales, they also represent powerful mirrors of the society that created them. Through a lens of deep and thoughtful analysis, we will delve into these stories, revealing the profound connections between myth and reality, between the human and the divine, between the individual and the community.

The Social Interpretation of Cosmogony

Cosmogony, dear reader, is that branch of mythology concerning the birth of the universe and the creation of the world. Think of that magical moment when everything began, when the first lights and colors flashed into the void. In Greek myths, this is a moment of conflict and transformation, an epic struggle for power that ultimately gives birth to the world as we know it. Now imagine ancient Greek society, with its complicated power plays and its ongoing struggles for control of resources. Don't you see a reflection of this reality in the tale of cosmogony? The Titans, for example, represent an old generation of power, symbols of a previous era. Their struggle with the new gods, the Olympians, can be seen as a conflict between old and new, between what was and what will be. Zeus, the king of the gods, emerges as the ultimate victor in this battle. And his triumph is not just a cosmic event, but also represents the ideal of the strong and just leader who governs with wisdom and strength. Zeus thus becomes the symbol of good governance, the model to emulate for human leaders.

And finally, the creation of man. According to the myth of Prometheus, man was created from mud and received the gift of fire, symbolizing knowledge and civilization. This myth can be interpreted as a celebration of human progress, of ingenuity, and the ability to overcome difficulties. At the same time, Prometheus's punishment underscores the danger of defying the gods, a lesson in humility and respect for human limits.

Cosmogony, then, is much more than a story about the creation of the world. It's a reflection of the values, aspirations, and conflicts of ancient Greek society. It's as if the myths are telling us: "Look, this is who we are, this is where we come from, and these are the values we hold important." It's a message that still resonates today, after thousands of years, because in the end, we are all, in one way or another, children of these myths.

Heroes and Demigods: Models of Human Virtues and Flaws

The heroes and demigods of Greek myths are much more than simple characters in ancient stories. They are mirrors of the values, ambitions, and fears of Greek society. In their stories, we see reflected the struggle for excellence, the desire for glory, the pursuit of wisdom, but also the awareness of human limits and the dangers of pride and arrogance. Through their adventures and their failures, the myths teach us valuable lessons about the challenges and rewards of human life.

The Twelve Labors of Hercules: Symbolism and Social Values

Hercules is perhaps the most famous hero of Greek mythology. His twelve labors, from untamable lions to monstrous hydras, represent more than mere physical challenges. They are symbols of endurance, courage, and the ongoing struggle between order and chaos. In Hercules, we see the Greek ideal of arete, excellence in all things, but we also see the torment of a man forced to serve, to pay the penalty for an unintentional crime.

Achilles and Immortal Glory

Do you remember Achilles, the indomitable hero of the Trojan War? He is a symbol of glory and courage, but also a reminder of human fragility.

Achilles chooses a brief but glorious life instead of a long anonymous one, showing the importance Greeks placed on fame and honor. However, his devastating wrath and his intransigence remind us that even the greatest heroes can fall due to their flaws.

Odysseus and Wisdom as a Fundamental Value

Then there's Odysseus, the hero of the long journey home after the Trojan War. More than any other hero, Odysseus symbolizes wisdom, ingenuity, and persistence. His cunning in overcoming trials, from the sirens to Polyphemus, is an example of the Greek valuation of intelligence as a fundamental virtue. But Odysseus has his flaws, including arrogance and temptation, which prolong his journey and put his life and those of his companions at risk.

Women in Greek Myths: Figures of Power and Tragedy

Women in Greek myths are not merely supporting characters, but often are at the center of the narrative. Through their stories, we can better understand the roles and values of women in ancient Greek society, as well as the conflicts and tensions that could arise. Whether they are faithful wives, fierce avengers, or seductive goddesses, these women represent the complexity and diversity of female experience in a male-dominated society. Their stories remind us that even in a world of heroes and gods, women's voices and experiences play a vital role.

Penelope and the Ideal of Fidelity

Let's start with Penelope, the devoted wife of Odysseus. While Odysseus is away, engaged in his epic journey, Penelope stays at home, resisting the courtship of numerous suitors and remaining faithful to her absent husband. Her cleverness in keeping the suitors at bay with the ruse of the loom is a symbol of cunning and wisdom, values highly esteemed in Greek society. Penelope represents the ideal of fidelity and patience, showing a kind of strength that is no less heroic than that of Odysseus.

Medea and Revenge as a Response to the Violation of the Sacred Marital Bond

Then there's Medea, a figure of great power and great tragedy. When her husband Jason betrays her, Medea responds with a terrible revenge that includes the killing of her own children. The myth of Medea highlights the power of women and the terror it can arouse, but also represents the sanctity of marriage and the consequences of its violation.

Aphrodite and the Role of Love and Beauty in Greek Society

Aphrodite, the goddess of love and beauty, is a central figure in Greek mythology. Her beauty is so potent that it causes conflicts among the gods, and her role in myths underscores the importance of love, desire, and beauty in Greek society. But Aphrodite is also a complex figure, capable of deceit and revenge when she is offended or neglected.

Myths as Reflection of Political and Social Structure

Navigating the waters of Greek mythology, we discover how myths can serve as a mirror of the political and social structure. The gods, heroes, monsters, all have a role in this grand stage that reflects the complexity of ancient Greek society.

City-states in Myths: Athens, Sparta, Thebes

When we think of ancient Greece, we think of its famous city-states, or poleis: Athens, Sparta, Thebes. Each of these cities has a starring role in Greek myths. Athens, for example, is the city protected by the goddess Athena, symbol of wisdom and strategic skill. Athenian myths reflect these values, showing how wisdom can triumph over brute power. Sparta, on the other hand, is famous for its militarization and discipline, and its myths often reflect these aspects. Thebes, known for its tragic stories of family conflict, like that of Oedipus, reminds us of the complexity and fragility of human life.

The Gods and Political Dynamics: Zeus as a Symbol of Leadership

In Greek mythology, Zeus is the king of the gods, the undisputed leader of Olympus. But his leadership is not always peaceful, and he often has to face revolts and challenges. These myths reflect the dynamics of power in Greek society, where leadership was a matter of balance between strength and wisdom, between authority and consensus. Zeus, with his triumphs and his failures, becomes a model of leadership, showing both its potential and its dangers.

Social Contradictions in Myths: Wealth, Poverty, and Power

Greek myths do not hide the contradictions of society. Myths such as those of Midas, the king who turns everything he touches into gold, or Narcissus, the handsome youth who falls in love with his own image, tell us about the dangers of wealth, beauty, and power. They show us that excess in everything can lead to ruin, and that true values, like wisdom, humility, and love, are much more precious.

The Social Interpretation of Conflict and Cooperation in Myths

Finally, Greek myths reflect social dynamics of conflict and cooperation. The struggles between gods, between heroes, between city-states, are all reflections of the tensions that can arise in a society. At the same time, the myths also speak of alliances, of friendship, of love, showing how cooperation can lead to results that force alone cannot achieve.

Rituals and Ceremonies: Religion as an Integral Part of Daily Life

The rituals and ceremonies of ancient Greece were rich and profound traditions that represented a fundamental aspect of daily life, showing how religion permeated every aspect of Greek society. Through these practices, the Greeks honored the gods, celebrated community life, sought answers to their doubts, and faced the reality of death. Religion, therefore, was not just a matter of beliefs, but a way of living, a fabric that united society and gave meaning and purpose to individual life.

The Gods and Daily Worship: A Constant Presence

The Greek gods were not just mythical figures, they were a constant presence in the daily lives of the Greeks. Every home had its household altar, every city its temples. The gods were honored with daily prayers, offerings, and sacrifices. This daily practice reflected the sense of respect and religious duty that characterized Greek society.

Festivals and Celebrations: From the Olympic Games to the Dionysia

Festivals were another key moment of Greek worship. These celebrations, often linked to the cycles of nature and the myths of the gods, were moments of joy and sharing. Consider the Olympic Games, the famous games in honor of Zeus, or the Dionysia, the spring festivals dedicated to the god of wine and frenzy. These celebrations were not just occasions for fun, but were also a way to strengthen community bonds and to remember the fundamental values and myths of society.

Oracles and Predictions: The Search for Answers

Oracles, like the one at Delphi, were an important element of Greek religion. People turned to these sacred places to seek answers, advice, forecasts for the future. This practice shows how the Greeks sought in religion a guide for the uncertainties and dilemmas of life.

Death and the Afterlife: Funeral Rites and Beliefs About Destiny After Death

Death, of course, was another important aspect of religious life. Greek funeral rites were rich and varied, showing deep respect for the deceased and concern for their fate in the afterlife. The stories of Hades, the god of the underworld, and his mysterious realms, underline the Greeks' fear but also curiosity in the face of the mystery of death.

Myths and Philosophy: The Influence of Mythological Thinking on Early Forms of Greek Philosophy

Greek philosophy not only used myth, but also offered a new interpretation of traditional myths. Philosophers like Plato and Aristotle examined myths in the light of reason, trying to extract philosophical or ethical truths from them. In this way, Greek philosophy and Greek mythology nourished each other, creating a single, rich fabric of thought and imagination.

The Myth as a Primitive Form of Explaining the World

Greek myths, with their fascinating stories of gods, heroes, and monsters, were much more than simple fantastical tales. They were a way for the ancient Greeks to explain the world around them, to make sense of natural phenomena, to explore the complex interweavings of human life, and to provide a moral framework in which to live. Lightning was not just an electrical discharge, but a symbol of Zeus's power. The arrival of spring was not just a seasonal change, but a celebration of Persephone's rebirth. This is the beauty of myth: it combines imagination, nature, and morality into one engaging narrative.

The Presocratics and the Transition from Myth to Reason

But with the arrival of the Presocratics, we see a turn in Greek thought. Philosophers like Thales, Anaximander, and Heraclitus began to seek more rational explanations of the world, based on logic rather than myth. But they did not completely reject myth. On the contrary, they used mythological thinking as a springboard for their new approach. For example, Anaximander spoke of the Apeiron, a concept that combined the mythological idea of chaos with a rational understanding of the infinite.

Plato and Mythology: The Cave as a Philosophical Myth

Even Plato, one of the greatest philosophers of antiquity, made extensive use of myths. But Plato's myths were different: they were philosophical myths, designed to explore and explain philosophical concepts. Take, for example, the myth of the cave, one of Plato's most famous allegories. This story, which talks about prisoners who only see shadows on the wall of a cave, is a powerful tool to explore themes such as reality, knowledge, and philosophical enlightenment.

CHAPTER 7

The Impact of Greek Mythology on Modern Civilization

Greek Mythology in Today's World

Greek mythology, with its epic tales and grand pantheon, continues to echo through our lives today. You've probably heard of The Odyssey, or about the remarkable feats of heroes like Hercules, and the divine mischief of gods like Zeus. You might wonder, however, why these ancient tales still matter in our modern world.

Believe it or not, these intriguing narratives from the Greeks still carry profound significance. Let's start with the fact that the Greeks were a profoundly insightful civilization. They were avid explorers of knowledge, forever curious and constantly pushing the boundaries of their understanding. Their literature isn't just filled with tales about gods and their divine deeds. Instead, it offers us a fascinating window into how the ancient Greeks perceived their world and moral universe.

Did you know the term "myth" itself originates from the ancient Greek language? It roughly translates to "word" or "story." Interestingly, this word doesn't imply something false or imaginary. Indeed, the Greeks crafted their narratives on the foundation of their observed realities. When we interpret myths in this light, they morph into more than just riveting tales about mythical beings. They become historical texts waiting for us to unravel their deeper truths.

Greek mythology is filled with narratives of intelligent characters who occasionally succumb to foolish mistakes. From these stories, we can extract timeless life lessons that still hold true today. They serve as reminders of virtues like patience, kindness, and forgiveness.

So, while you might think of Greek myths as merely fascinating ancient stories, remember they are also mirrors reflecting human nature and our shared human history. The Greeks weren't just telling tales; they were exploring the complexities of existence, a task we continue to grapple with even in today's world.

Greek Influence in Everyday Life

Everyday life is rich with traces of Greek mythology, sometimes in places you'd least expect. For example, take a look at some of the brands you encounter daily. The famous sports brand Nike didn't just spring out of thin air - it was named after Nike, the Greek goddess of victory. You might also be surprised to find out that Midas, the car service company, drew inspiration from the Greek myth of King Midas.

Ever flipped through an atlas, scanning over maps of the world? You have Greek mythology to thank for that term too! In these stories, Atlas was a mighty Titan tasked by Zeus to bear the weight of the sky for eternity following the Titans' defeat by the Olympians. In honor of this mythological titan's burden, we've named our map books "atlases."

Greek mythology has also made quite a splash in the world of cinema. Think about movies like Troy, Hercules, and Clash of the Titans. These films draw heavily from the captivating tales spun by the Greeks. And let's not forget about the plethora of monstrous and otherworldly creatures from Greek myths that regularly pop up in contemporary films and books.

So you see, no matter how many centuries have passed since the Greeks first spun tales of their gods and heroes, their stories continue to captivate us. These ancient narratives have woven themselves into the fabric of our daily lives, adding a sprinkle of mythological magic to our modern world.

The Influence of Greek Drama

The tradition of public discourse, oratory, and dramatic presentation established in classical Greece has left an indelible imprint on the world's understanding of Greek mythology. This culture of performance was rooted in celebrations dedicated to the god Dionysus, an intriguing figure in the Greek pantheon. Dionysus is said to be "twice-born," stemming from his unique birth story involving his mortal mother Semele and Zeus, the king of gods. His colorful life, filled with adventure, danger, and even resurrection, earned him the affection of Zeus and the disdain of Hera, Zeus' wife.

Dionysus was widely associated with viticulture, fertility, wine, ritual madness, pleasure, festivity, parties, and, of course, theater. His sacred animals include the leopard, lynx, and tiger, along with the erotically potent goat, a symbol embodied by satyrs, mythical creatures that are half-man, half-goat. He was known as a traveling god, frequently traversing far and wide, and acquiring a reputation as Olympus' "bad boy."

Numerous festivals honoring Dionysus were held throughout ancient Greece, all marked by grand celebrations filled with eating, drinking, dancing, and communal merriment. Of these, the most significant was the City Dionysia, held annually in Athens from March 9th to 13th. It was a prominent literary competition, attracting the best writers of the era, particularly dramatists.

Aeschylus, a notable tragedian who lived between 525 and 456 BCE, was a frequent participant and victor at the Dionysia. Out of his extensive body of work, seven plays survive today. He also revealed the initiation rituals of the Eleusinian Mysteries through his works, which sparked an assassination attempt on his life while performing on stage.

Sophocles, another legendary tragedian, further revolutionized Greek drama by increasing the number of actors in a play, transforming it into an interactive dramatic performance. He authored over 100 plays, with seven surviving in their entirety. Notably, his work "Electra," about Agamemnon's daughter seeking revenge on her mother and her mother's lover for Agamemnon's murder, is one of his most compelling tragedies.

Euripides, born in 480 BCE, was another prolific poet and dramatist who entered the City Dionysia in 455 BCE. He wrote about 90 plays, 17 of which are still in existence. He is known for his complex female characters such as Medea, Hecuba, and Andromache. His play "The Bacchae" is a profound exploration of the conflict between reason and irrationality, centered on Dionysus' return to Thebes.

Importantly, the Dionysia mandated that every participating writer should present at least one satirical play or substantial comedy. Aristophanes, who lived around 456-380 BCE, was a masterful comedy writer, best remembered for his sharp social and political satire in plays like "The Birds," "The Clouds," and "Lysistrata." These works still resonate today, reminding us of the timeless power and influence of Greek drama.

The Origins of Greek Civilization

The beginnings of Greek civilization, which undeniably marked the dawn of Europe's first civilization, remain steeped in mystery. Nestled in the heart of the Mediterranean, the fertile island of Crete presented an ideal environment for the rise of an early civilization. Its prime position in the middle of trade routes and its natural protection from invasion due to its island status made it a beacon for early settlers. However, it remains unclear who exactly can be credited for bringing civilization to this fortunate isle. Some theories point towards individuals from Asia Minor, while others attribute it to the adventurous Egyptian merchants, emphasizing their advanced seafaring skills even in the earliest days of the second millennium.

The civilization that sprouted on Crete, however, was unlike any of the grand empires in the Ancient Near East. Unlike the territorial states of Egypt, Babylon, and later the Hittites, which relied heavily on agriculture, military power, and political centralization, Crete was a commercial empire. Its power was derived from its mastery over the seas, a concept so unique that it was called a "thalassocracy".

Crete's prosperity hinged on the Aegean Sea, which in the third millennium became a sprawling marketplace dotted with villages and towns along the Anatolian coast and the neighboring islands. Egypt, which was already highly civilized, traded its finely crafted products with these coastal settlements, receiving timber and other raw materials in return. This trade was facilitated by the unique geography of the Aegean, which, abundant in islands and islets, provided ample navigation points and landmarks for the sailors (navigation in that era was primarily by sight, relying on the sailors' memory of the coastlines).

As trade in the eastern Mediterranean surged, so did Crete's fortune. The island's influence expanded concurrently with the growth and enrichment of the Near East empires. From its bloom around 2300 BC until its decline around 1400 BC, Crete served as the commercial middleman for these grand empires, amassing vast wealth in the process. Thus, despite its origins being shrouded in uncertainty, the impact of the first European civilization on Crete resonates throughout the annals of history.

Cretan Civilization and Minoan Civilization

The rich and enigmatic history of Crete, spanning a millennium, can be broken down into three prominent phases, each possessing its unique character and dramatic incidents.

The first phase, known as the palatial period (2300-1700 BC), set the foundation of Crete's civilization with the building of the first palaces in the island's principal cities. Intriguingly, the low military relevance of these structures suggests that conflicts among the cities were probably rare. It was during this period of booming commerce that Crete established itself as a prominent commercial power. However, around 1700 BC, the civilization inexplicably crumbled, with buildings deserted and falling into ruin. The potential causes behind this sudden downfall are still a matter of debate among scholars, with a large earthquake being a plausible explanation.

Following the collapse, Crete entered the second phase or the neopalatial period (1700-1400 BC). This was a time of revival, beginning with the reconstruction of the ravaged structures and the rejuvenation of trade. During this period, Crete's civilization reached a zenith of splendor, leaving even the courts of Egypt and Babylon in awe. It also saw the development of the Linear A writing system, likely inspired by Egyptian hieroglyphics.

The third phase (1400-1200 BC) bore witness to the abrupt end of Cretan civilization. The sudden collapse was akin to a jolt from deep sleep for the ruling class, followed by an invasion by the Mycenaeans, a Peloponnesian population. Once again, theories proposed to explain this swift downfall included the possibility of a catastrophic tidal wave. Crete never regained its former glory after falling under the rule of the Mycenaeans.

Despite the dramatic changes in leadership, the day-to-day life of Crete's peasant population saw little disruption. The societal structure remained intact; peasants still lived on the bare essentials while funneling everything else to the palace. The impact of Cretan civilization's downfall was more profound externally; the Phoenicians inherited Crete's role, becoming the dominant force in the Mediterranean trade routes for centuries to follow.

Surprisingly, much about the Cretan civilization remains unknown due to the yet-to-be-deciphered Linear A and the disappearance of spoken language by the middle of the first millennium. What we do know stems from indirect sources such as Egypt and the stunning frescoes that continue to adorn the walls of the majestic ruins, offering a vivid glimpse of the past grandeur.

The lack of defensive structures indicates that life on Crete was relatively peaceful. In the neopalatial phase, even rudimentary defensive features like ditches disappeared, suggesting that a single sovereign probably ruled the entire island. The ruins of the buildings hint at a lively and sophisticated craft industry, indicating a luxurious lifestyle for the ruling class.

The social structure of Crete mirrors the temple-palace model, familiar among ancient Mesopotamian societies like the Sumerians and Egyptians. This model consolidated political, religious, and economic power within a grand palace, home to the king, priests, nobles, soldiers, and artisans. Peasants, scattered across the countryside, depended on the palace for their needs. Profits from maritime trade, a unique feature of the Cretan civilization, were likely managed by the palace and used to expand trade routes or construct extravagant buildings, adding further opulence to the island's landscape.

The religious practices of ancient Crete appear to have roots in the Neolithic era, as evidenced by anthropomorphic deities and a tendency towards fetishism. The people saw divinity in the magic of natural phenomena such as lightning or magnetic stones and revered ancient caves or majestic trees as sacred spaces. These religious traditions, like Mount Ida—later known as Zeus's childhood home in Greek mythology—or the Mother Goddess symbolizing love and fertility—later reborn as Aphrodite—were adopted by the Greeks in later centuries.

Crete holds a unique place in history as the birthplace of the first civilization on European soil. It emerged, flourished, and vanished within the second millennium, and was remarkably distinct compared to its Mesopotamian and Egyptian contemporaries. Moreover, Cretan civilization was instrumental in kickstarting the civilization of the Peloponnese, where they likely established trading ports.

A significant aspect of Cretan influence was the imparting of civilian, technical, and cultural knowledge to the Mycenaeans, a Peloponnesian population that later became crucial in Greek history. For a long time, Mycenaeans were considered an offshoot of Cretan civilization until English archaeologist Michael Ventris deciphered Linear B in 1952, refuting this assumption.

The most well-known tale tying the two civilizations together is that of Minos, the king of Knossos—the heart of Cretan civilization—and the Minotaur. This relationship between the Mycenaeans and the Cretans would dramatically reverse around 1400 BC with the Mycenaean conquest of Crete.

Much about the Cretan civilization remains a mystery today, although its high-level achievements are evident in the remnants of its grand buildings. Its influence on Greek history is underappreciated, despite the fact that Crete was a beacon of civilization when mainland Greece was still in prehistory. Cretan civilization traded with these primitive societies, likely sharing much of their knowledge.

While it's clear that the Cretans were not Greeks, they played a pivotal role in the civilization of what would later become Ancient Greece. As a result, not just the Greeks, but Western civilizations at large, owe a great deal to the Cretans.

So closely connected were the Cretan and Mycenaean civilizations that they're sometimes collectively referred to as the Cretan-Mycenaean civilization. The Peloponnese was the birthplace of the Mycenaean civilization, where trade with Crete was intense.

Unlike Crete, where the temple-palace and trade were central, the Mycenaean civilization was characterized by a society built around agriculture and pastoralism. While the palace was the center of political and military organization in Mycenaean centers, an agricultural aristocracy also emerged. Over time, the differences between the two civilizations became more pronounced.

The Mycenaeans fortified their centers and organized themselves into small, autonomous military states. Around 1400 BC, when the Cretan civilization collapsed abruptly, the Mycenaeans launched an invasion of Crete, marking a turning point in their history. Despite never being able to restore Crete to its former glory, this conquest represented a new phase of Mycenaean expansion, allowing them to extend their influence to the main islands of the Aegean and regions of central Greece, and culminating in the famed destruction of Troy, immortalized in the Iliad.

CONCLUSION

As we conclude our journey through the enthralling world of Greek mythology, it is our hope that these captivating tales of gods, heroes, and fantastical creatures have not only entertained you but have also provided you with a deeper understanding of the Greek culture and way of thinking. By exploring these myths, we have discovered that despite the passage of millennia, their underlying themes and lessons continue to resonate in our modern lives.

We hope that the stories within these pages have ignited your imagination and inspired you to see the world through the eyes of the ancient Greeks. The lessons they imparted on love, courage, wisdom, and the human condition hold a timeless relevance that transcends the boundaries of history and culture.

It is our sincerest wish that your experience with this book has been enriching and enlightening, leaving you with a newfound appreciation for the impact of Greek mythology on contemporary thought and art. May you carry the spirit of these myths with you as you continue on your own personal odyssey through life, ever mindful of the wisdom and beauty that can be found in the stories of our ancestors.

Before we part ways, we would like to extend our deepest gratitude to you, dear reader, for embarking on this incredible journey with us. Your curiosity, passion, and eagerness to explore the realms of Greek mythology have been the driving force behind this book. We are truly grateful for your presence and engagement, and it has been an honor to share these stories with you.

In addition, we would like to acknowledge the countless scholars, translators, and researchers whose tireless efforts have made it possible for us to enjoy and appreciate the richness of Greek mythology today. Their dedication to preserving and understanding these ancient tales has ensured that the legacy of the ancient Greeks continues to endure and inspire.

Finally, we would like to thank our families, friends, and colleagues for their unwavering support and encouragement throughout the creation of this book. Your belief in our vision has been instrumental in bringing these timeless stories to life for a new generation of readers.

As you close this book and venture forth, may the myths and legends of ancient Greece continue to inspire, guide, and enthral you in your own life's journey. Farewell, dear reader, and may the wisdom of the ancients be with you always!

Dear Reader...

Our literary adventure has come to an end, at least for this book... Writing the manual you are holding in your hands has been a wonderful opportunity to challenge ourselves and open our hearts. We have put down on paper all our passion and experience gained in this field...

We hope that our company has intrigued and informed you, and that you have found useful insights and tools in the previous pages to develop your curiosity and passion for Greek Mythology and, as a result, to grow as a person and embody the values that make you unique and incomparable. Don't rush your learning; this is a journey that requires a lot of practice and commitment, but it should not stop you from achieving your goals.

Remember, the secret to an exciting and fulfilling life is to enjoy the journey.

If this is the case for you and you have found this book useful in any way, it would be fantastic if you could leave sincere feedback on Amazon to help us grow and spread our message to as many people as possible. We wish you all the best and have a good life!

Scan below to leave a review for this book

Greetings,

Inkwell House Press

78815837R00077